DE-RISKING
THE
NGO

CORDELL ASHLEY PAYNE

INDIA • SINGAPORE • MALAYSIA

Notion Press

Old No. 38, New No. 6
McNichols Road, Chetpet
Chennai - 600 031

First Published by Notion Press 2020
Copyright © Cordell Ashley Payne 2020
All Rights Reserved.

ISBN 978-1-64828-705-3

"The best intentions are nullified by unmitigated risk"

– Cordell Ashley Payne

This book is dedicated to

Alexa Shannon Payne and Lancy Maria Payne

Contents

Preface

There are many out there who will wonder about the rationale of writing such a book, on what can evidently be categorised as a "niche" segment in our economy.

As a professional with nigh on 2 decades of work experience, I have had the privilege of serving close to 10 years in the banking industry (with 3 different private sector "new generation" banks) and the rest of my tenure with NGOs/social sector organisations. While I have worked directly as a senior-level employee with 2 such entities, I have had the opportunity to assist and/or function in an advisory capacity (from time-to-time) with no less than 5 such organisations – thereby being witness to the various styles of functioning. Coming from the cutting-edge professional side of the fence to the NGO side (and making a comparison between the two sides of the coin), I cannot help but quote Mark Twain here as in "East is East and West is West, and ne'er the twain shall meet".

One notes many "minor" infractions and, in some cases, some horrifyingly serious lapses – lapses which, in the corporate world, would result in the perpetrator of the offence being summarily hanged, drawn and quartered. Your "severed" head would be mounted on a spike at the city gates – as an example to others not to make similar mistakes. Yet, such infractions and lapses often don't seem to warrant a sleepless night in the NGO. It would be ethically incorrect to be a Pontius Pilate and wash my hands off and even more inappropriate, to do nothing but express regret and merely repeat those famous words (of Jesus Christ) "Father, forgive them, for they know not what they do".

Should the NGO/social service organisation function on the "blunt-edge of the knife" and be exempted from all statutory/regulatory compliances, merely because their objectives are purely altruistic? *Should such entities operate at the opposite end of the managerial spectrum from corporates, in their efficiency of functioning?* Can't such organisations be run on similar "cutting-edge" methods/procedures as corporates? <u>Why ever not?</u> Why downgrade yourselves and be content with the mis-perception of being the "poor and downtrodden cousins of the corporates?". Heck, the fact of the matter (and stark reality) is NGOs do more noble work than corporates do. If it were not for the (recent) mandatory CSR rules under the Indian Companies Act, the vast majority of corporates would do diddly-squat, to benefit the poorer & underprivileged sections of our society.

Indeed, <u>corporates make profits but *NGOs change lives*</u>!

There are numerous avenues/functional areas in NGOs, where we take our current practices for granted – content to ride our luck (and our charitable status)! Leadership, in our NGOs, needs to learn & adopt professional styles of management and modern managerial methods, as well as corporate accountability and responsibility practices.

Let's take a lot of leaves out of the corporate management book and run our social sector entities the way the corporate leadership run theirs.

Change the way you go about changing society!

Chapter I

What is Risk?

There are a great many books written on the concept of risk and risk management – both in India and the world at large. Risk is a concept that pervades and affects almost all aspects of human life – whether health, wealth, education, government, relationships, family, business, industry, travel, and so on.

The very essence of risk is negativity. In other words, risk connotes some degree of the negative.

If one were to define risk, some definitions would be as follows.

The online "Business Dictionary" Defines Risk As

1. A probability or threat of damage, injury, liability, loss, or any other negative occurrence that is caused by external or internal vulnerabilities, and that may be avoided through pre-emptive action.

2. Finance: The probability that an actual return on an investment will be lower than the expected return. Financial risk is divided into the following categories: Basic risk, Capital risk, Country risk, Default risk, Delivery risk, Economic risk, Exchange rate risk, Interest rate risk, Liquidity risk, Operations risk, Payment system risk, Political risk, Refinancing risk, Reinvestment risk, Settlement risk, Sovereign risk, and Underwriting risk.

3. Food industry: The possibility that due to a certain hazard in food there will be a negative effect to a certain magnitude.

4. Insurance: A situation where the probability of a variable (such as burning down of a building) is known but when a mode of occurrence or the actual value of the occurrence (whether the fire will occur at a particular property) is not.

    A risk is not an uncertainty (where neither the probability nor the mode of occurrence is known), a peril (cause of loss), or a hazard (something that makes the occurrence of a peril more likely or more severe).

5. Securities trading: The probability of a loss or drop in value. Trading risk is divided into two general categories: (1) Systemic risk affects all securities in the same class and is linked to the overall capital-market system and therefore cannot be eliminated by diversification. Also called market risk. (2) Nonsystematic risk is any risk that isn't market-related or is not systemic. Also called nonmarket risk, extra-market risk, or unsystemic risk.

6. Workplace: Product of the consequence and probability of a hazardous event or phenomenon.

(Source: http://www.businessdictionary.com/definition/risk.html)

The Merriam-Webster Dictionary Defines Risk As
Definition of risk

1) Possibility of loss or injury: <u>PERIL</u>

2) someone or something that creates or suggests a hazard

3) **a.** the chance of loss or the perils to the subject matter of an insurance contract; *also*: the degree of probability of such loss

    b. a person or thing that is a specified hazard to an insurer

    c. an insurance hazard from a specified cause or source war *risk*

4) the chance that an investment (such as a stock or commodity) will lose value

The Oxford Living Dictionary Defines Risk As

NOUN

1. A situation involving exposure to danger.

VERB

[WITH OBJECT]

1. Expose (someone or something valued) to danger, harm, or loss.

Well, then, what is risk?

If I were to summarise from all three dictionary definitions, _risk is the_ **_possibility or probability_** _of loss or damage; or_ **_exposure_** _to a potentially dangerous/hazardous situation; any of which_ **_may_** _threaten life, commerce, profit, etc._

That's a simplistic definition. Now let's have a look at what some of the noteworthy management authors/management gurus have to say about risk.

At this juncture, I must add an adequate dose of caution before we can go the whole hog on risk and its consequences. Risk is a PROBABILITY or POSSIBILITY of something negative happening or the occurrence of a negative situation. It is NOT A REALITY.

A risk is a probability is a probability is a probability......

However, this is just the scenario in black and white. Now let's add the colour of consequence to this picture.

Somehow, let's say, out of thin air that 'distant' probability suddenly takes the shape and form of reality. What follows next is full-blown CONSEQUENCE!!

Result: Your best intentions lie shattered on the jagged rocks of consequence.

Each and every individual (and organisation) has to choose whether to acknowledge the presence of risk and finds ways to mitigate it or to be like the proverbial ostrich and bury the head in the sand – refusing to acknowledge the threat of danger.

As an author, I cannot address the way of the ostrich, and choose instead the way of the former – that of risk and the mitigation of it.

The eminent management thinker *Peter Drucker* said of risk:

"Tomorrow always arrives. It is always different. And even the mightiest company is in trouble if it has not worked on the future. Being surprised by what happens is a risk that even the largest and richest company cannot afford, and even the smallest business need not run."[1]

It is extremely interesting to note that in his above remark, Drucker says that "…even the mightiest company is in trouble if it has not worked on the future." In other words, nobody, not even Apple, Samsung, Ferrari, Tata Consultancy Services, Reliance Industries, or any other corporate entity can afford to take their future for granted or ignore the risks that the future poses.

Drucker, on risk, also went on to say

"Most innovators are successful to the extent to which they define risks and confine them."[2]

(1 & 2: Source: https://www.azquotes.com/author/4147-Peter_Drucker/tag/risk)

Going by Peter Drucker's quote, the successful innovator is one who is able to define risk & confine it. This quality is therefore the differentiator between the successful innovator, the failed innovator and the "for-a-while-successful-innovator".

However, it is essential here that we must pose the question – why does Drucker speak of confining risk, can't we eliminate risk altogether? For the answer to that, let's look to another management guru – Alvin Toffler, the eminent author of books such as Future Shock, Third Wave, Power Shift, etc.

Alvin Toffler, in his interview to Popular Science in September 2002 said:

"I think we have to accept risk in our lives. You cannot eliminate all risk without being dead."

(Source: https://www.popsci.com/future-shock-author-alvin-toffler-dead-at-87)

Toffler's words point unequivocally to what I refer to as '**the constancy of risk**'. Risk is undeniable and cannot be wished away. Deny it three times if you will – ultimately the 'proverbial cock will crow', revealing the falseness of the denial. Risk is constant – existing in all spheres of life. Driving across a bridge carries with it the risk of the bridge collapsing. Merely walking down a road carries with it the risk of accident or injury. Simply staying home to avoid external risk carries with it risk itself – the risk of fire, risk of heart-attack, earthquake and house collapse, etc. Risk is constant and all pervading.

Touché! (you say). You concede the point on constancy of risk.

And then, you might say – "risk and the NGO?" NGOs are traditionally thought of as "risk-free" environments or entities. After all they don't take risk, they don't indulge in risky activities or risky investments. NGOs operate in the social sector – helping people with skill development, healthcare, education, self-help-groups, etc. Where is the risk in such activities?

Hidden – indeed, very well hidden and quite often discovered too late to make amends or neutralise or even confine.

Revisiting my words of a couple of paragraphs before, the constancy of risk therefore necessitates that risk applies to ALL – even the social sector (or the NGO world, if you may). We live and operate in a dynamic environment with the goal posts being shifted constantly and the boundary lines being drawn and re-drawn by circumstances, external agents and factors & developments uncontrollable by us or our governing body/bodies. Each passing day brings a new 'D-factor' or 'disruption factor' with it – seemingly innocuous things and events that shift the goalposts & redraw the boundary lines. Counted among these D-factors are things like regulatory changes, the Donald Trumps of global governments, foreign exchange fluctuations, oil-on-the-boil, humanitarian crises in pockets across the globe, climate change and oh, so much more. All one needs to do is to flip the pages of any newspaper or browse news channels for an hour and the 'breaking news' D-factors stare you in the face.

The greatest tragedy, however, is that we social sector types choose to 'in-seeing-not-see' that which stares us in the face, the existence of ever present & future risk. We adopt the 'Ostrich posture' – burying our heads in the sand, gloriously oblivious (whether deliberately or unwittingly) of the goings-on around us, in what can only be classified as the Nero syndrome. (Nero – the Roman emperor is rumoured to have played a fiddle-like instrument while Rome burnt in 70 A.D)

For us, the philosophy we seem to live by is 'Ceteris Paribus' (Latin for 'other conditions remaining the same/constant'). Possibly we 'NGO-ites' choose to dwell in a utopian world, where we believe that all other factors shall remain constant and nothing and no-one can disrupt our model of functioning – never giving a thought to the 'D-factors' and their being the harbingers of risk and consequence.

The reality is, oh so, different. A simple thing such as the movement of the foreign exchange conversion rate – which happens from day to day & minute to minute – affects our NGO's funds, if we are the recipient of foreign donations/foreign grants & support. To illustrate – a 1 Rupee movement per dollar (positive or negative) for a US $ 10000 donation, can translate into Rs. 10000 more for a project or Rs. 10000 less for a project. Money which can pay one person's salary for a month or defray 10% of a Rs. 100,000 budget or cause a 10% deficit? It's an example of a D-factor which can determine a financial surplus or a deficit.

RISK – can we afford to ignore it?

This book dwells on some of the many kinds of risk that an NGO or social sector organisation may face in the course of its day to day functioning, and it seeks to provide a few solutions to de-risking the business or mitigating (not eliminating) the risks.

Chapter II

Types of Risk for an NGO

Every NGO or social sector organisation is subject to a wide variety of risks – almost the same as any small or mid-size corporate. While the mid to large size company has/may have skilled professionals/resource persons to anticipate, deal with or manage and mitigate such risk, most NGOs have little or no access to the services of such professionals/skilled people.

So, what does an NGO and its management do in order to manage and mitigate risk? The very first step in that process would be to know what risks their organisation faces – a sort of THREAT analysis, as it were.

Let's begin there, shall we? Without further delay, let us then sink our teeth into the crux of this risk pie. What risks can an NGO face in its day to day conduct of business/operations?

These risks are widespread and range from financial risk to operational risk; from donor risk to human risk to automation risk to government risk and so on.

In this chapter, let's begin by listing some of the risk areas for an NGO or social sector/third sector organisation and will briefly provide an overview of potential risks emanating from that risk area, before progressing to discuss each risk area in much detail in the subsequent, separate chapters.

Financial Risk – As the name suggests, this has to do with the risks related to Finance and financial management in the NGO. It encompasses risks related to the amount of cash we hold from day to day; skill levels for managing finances; risks arising out of banking knowledge or rather lack of it; risks related to foreign exchange, etc.

Operational & Procedural Risk – This risk area has to do with the risks arising from our operational procedures in our organisations. How do we operate? Do we operate in a rather loose, unstructured manner, with very high degrees of centralization or do we have a structured hierarchy to manage things? Do we have a process orientation or is our core management philosophy that of 'adhocism'? For the running of our organisation do we have crystal clear methodology or do we frequently employ 'muddle-ology'? Are we faced with 'a management-crisis-a-day' or a crisis-a-month? The answers to each of these questions will provide you with an indication as to the level of operational and procedural risk in your organisation.

Donor Risk – Yes, indeed – donor risk. Surely a donor to your project/ organisation cannot be construed as a risk (irrespective of their country) – they would have to be categorised as your best friend. In reality, this is probably one of the areas of greatest concern for an NGO – because donors constitute among the highest degrees of risk to any non-profit organisation. We never seem to consider that the funding tap can be turned off at the drop of a hat or the turn of a whim.

Taxation Risk – The name itself says it all. "Beware – the taxman cometh". Which country of the world has no taxation policy or taxation department? If there were such a country, every corporate sector entity/NGO of the world would register/base itself there to buy itself peace from the taxman. Taxation is probably one of the biggest bugbears for the non-profit entity, which finds it difficult to deploy scarce financial resources to employ an experienced tax consultant or tax professional for tax compliance – in what is desperately needed expertise for negotiating the minefield.

FCRA Risks – In the Indian context, Non-profits receiving funds from foreign donors are subject to regulation by the government through the provisions of the Foreign Contribution Regulation Act (FCRA) 2010 (and earlier to the FCRA Act 1976). Most NGOs cannot wait to rush into the foreign funding territory (i.e. FCRA realm). In reality, this realm is one where most angels would fear to tread. Thick with regulations & reporting requirements, this sphere of NGO activity (for the uninitiated) is no less than a labyrinth placed in a minefield.

Human Intellectual Capital Risk/Human Resources risk – This is one risk area where NGOs, corporates and even educational institutions find themselves on the same plateau. The human risk factor – encompassing not having qualified staff or having too many staff or the risk of loss of what I refer to as 'Human Intellectual Capital'. People form the backbone of every organisation (even the tech companies) and the loss of key people or the lack of good people pose a large risk to the NGO.

Compliance & Legal Risk – Ten to fifteen years ago, NGOs were far less heavily regulated than they are today. With ever increasing violence, crime, corruption and terrorism the world over, there is a phenomenally high level of emphasis placed on regulatory compliance and the monitoring of NGOs. Increasing e-surveillance/e-monitoring measures adopted by government agencies have rendered statutory compliance ever more important.

Coupled with this is the ever-increasing knowledge level of individual rights. With smartphone penetration at all-time highs across the country, and cheap mobile internet connectivity, it takes a few seconds (minutes, at worst) to Google one's rights and obtain access to legal advice and redressal. Labour related litigation is one of the most common legal risks NGOs face today. In addition, there is a legal risk involved when an NGO seeks to acquire assets such as property.

Leadership Risk (managing teams and their one-downs) – The large majority of NGOs are handicapped with the absence of skilled leaders & managers. This in turn translates into the leadership risk arising from improper management of teams and leadership/mentoring of the leader's 'one-downs'. This risk cascades through the ranks, ultimately affecting adversely the NGOs output and its goal fulfilment.

Information Technology & Automation risk – All of us are quite familiar with how information technology has helped the world leap-frog many steps ahead. Gone are the days of the rotary dialling fixed line telephone, replaced by the mobile phone. Gone is the age old 'phone-calls-only' mobile phone to be replaced by the smartphone complete with voice, data, photography, advanced computing, etc.

In the tech world & e-commerce world today, there is much talk of 'disruptive technology'. Sounds paradoxical, doesn't it. After all, technology is meant to enable not disrupt. Disruptive technology is that which radically changes the way things have traditionally been done. Automations is one example of such technology – routine functions carried out by people being replaced by computers & software.

IT and automation can pose a serious risk to the way in which the NGO works or has traditionally worked. An entity doing the same social sector service the hi-tech way can put out of business a NGO doing the same service the traditional/manual way.

End-Result mapping & Goal Fulfilment Risk (done through systems & MIS) – Something that most of us NGO types do is to believe in the goal, raise the money, struggle through the difficulties, do the good work and start all over again – day in day out, month after month, year after year. Sometimes the awards & rewards come, most often they don't.

Very few spare a thought for tracking the end-results of their work through the use of Management Information Systems or MIS. When queried by donors on end-result achievements our answers tend to the intangible, skirting the measurable. Has the goal we set out to achieve been fulfilled? The reply is an emphatic yes without the quants (i.e. numbers) to back us up. The absence of end-result mapping and goal fulfilment measurement techniques most often result in the reality of donor risk.

Corporate Action Risk/Governmental Action Risk (Demo/GST)/ Judicial Consequence Risk – This is one risk factor over which the NGO has no control on whatsoever. This risk variable is of a purely external nature and often arises like a bolt from the blue. There may be warning signs at best though the consequences of such risk are industry-altering. From time to time governments resort to legislative changes or executive orders/actions and in doing so alter the sector's landscape altogether. The High Court/Supreme Court of the country may adjudicate on a Public Interest Litigation or a judicial matter of great national consequence and in doing so, pass a judgement with great ramification on the way our industry/sector functions.

Investment Risk – At some point in time or other, every NGO has surplus funds to park or invest, whether for the short term or long term. The very aspect of investment carries with it a degree of risk. To invest or not to invest but leave surplus funds idle in one's operational bank account? Shall we invest for less than 1 year, exactly 1 year, more than one year or five years? Where to invest – with banks, mutual funds, in real estate or some other investment avenue? The decisions that are associated with investing (or not investing) surplus funds carry with them varying degrees of risk. The trade-off between risk and return has to be considered before the final act. The act of investment does not signify the mitigation of the risk entirely as future risk becomes applicable.

Project – Planning & Implementation Risk (including sustainability risk) – Each social sector organisation/NGO has one or more projects through which they fulfil their social objective. Some have healthcare projects or hospitals or clinics, others have educational projects such as schools or skill development centres, even others have food sustenance programmes or substance abuse programmes.

Quite often programmes are initiated at the behest of the founder or even donor, with limited planning and much less focus on implementation. The planning and implementation stage for any project is absolutely crucial, as these are the two stages where the foundation, the functionality and even the future sustainability of the project are laid or 'cast in stone'. *If you plan to succeed, chances are you will but if you don't plan, you are surely planning to fail.*

Documentation risk (minutes, records, etc) – Merely because our organisations are in the social sector is no excuse or rationale for us not to adopt the best of corporate documentation standards. Must our organizations function on decisions conveyed by word-of-mouth and thereafter leave it to our weak memories to recollect who had said what and what was decided on DD/MM/YY? Very often, we do not adopt nor adhere to strong documentation standards or records of decisions, processes, minutes, approvals, etc, for future reference. In our present day and age of enhanced scrutiny & governmental monitoring, documentation can make the difference between and indictment and an acquittal. The best of social work and results lose their validity in the absence of records.

MYOPIA Risk – A good many people around us suffer from impaired eyesight – some of them from myopia (short-sightedness). Myopia in the NGO sense is the risk of leadership seeing only the short or medium term and not tuning in to the long term. It can result in a leader not wanting to takes decisions because he/she is not comfortable with any kind of blowback. Myopia can even be one man's autocracy in deciding on all & sundry. Whatever the case, it's a risk of the short term which can (most likely will) have at least one consequence in the long term.

This list of risks is by no means exhaustive. Whatever be the risk, the NGO must go the corporate way in order to survive & even thrive in today's dynamic scenario.

Manage the risk and thereby reduce or neutralize the consequence.

Chapter III

Financial Risk

Every manager, leader, entrepreneur and business person is aware of the fact that nothing in the commercial world moves without money. If commerce is the engine of industry, money is the fuel that powers it. Except that in the commercial world money is used for the generation of (more) money. In the social sector, in most cases, money is the fuel that powers the achievement of social/charitable objective/s.

With the absence of a focus on the 'profit' angle of the business or industry, the social sector has tended to (and tends to) forget the importance of efficient handling of money or finances. You see, it's all in the mind – it's the psychology of the matter. When chasing money, the efficiency of the chase and the ratio of the money invested to the money earned becomes crucial and often sworn by. Careers are made and even smashed on the jagged rocks of financial ratios.

The measures for this 'efficiency' are numerous and discussed on daily basis on business TV channels till the hosts can recite them in their sleep. The number crunchers possibly work 24×7 analysing corporate performance to boost investors' profits and their own company's revenue – in fact the number crunching is an industry in itself. In the corporate world, the indicators of financial & business performance are many. Just to name a few – Operating Profit Margin (OPM), Net Profit Margin (NPM), EBITDA (Earnings Before Interest, Tax, Depreciation & Amortisation), RONW (Return on Net Worth), ROCE (Return on Capital Employed), Gearing Ratio, and so on.

The success or failure of a company or business is measured largely in terms of these (and other) financial and performance ratios. The ratios imply the risk taken by that company and its degree of success in dealing with and mitigating those risks. All of them lead up (in some way or other) to and impact the risk-return ratio for investors & promoters.

There are no such financial or performance indicators for the NGO/social sector – making the managing of finances that much more difficult. Not only is the psychological obsession with financial efficiency missing, additionally there are negligible measures to follow through on such efficiency or the lack thereof.

The resultant effect is that managing finances in an NGO/social sector organisation becomes that much more difficult. You do not have a battery of ratios and efficiency parameters to tell you whether you are on the right track or on any track for that matter. Only when you know what you need or what you lack, can you make the effort to go out and acquire it or purchase it or even develop it. A situation which is aptly described in the words of Sir Francis Bacon – "Knowledge is power, ignorance is bliss."

In the absence of the obsession over right money management, we NGO types somehow blunder our way through the financial maze, tracing and re-tracing our steps – much like going round and round in circles in the desert on an extremely hot day.

Finance, in its essence, in an NGO is almost no different from that of a corporate – so is accounts. You have sources of funds, uses of funds, fund flows, receipts, payments, assets, liabilities, purchases, sales, ledgers, journals, accounting statements, etc. It encompasses budgeting for business periods and projects, receiving money on time, allocating financial resources to different avenues on an optimal basis, making payments at an optimal time, eliminating inflow-outflow mismatches (or Asset-Liability mismatches), foreign exchange aspects (if any), cash in hand, cash payments, banking transactions, liaison with banks, purchases, asset management, and so much more.

The vast (and ever-increasing role) of Finance and consequently Financial Management exposes every organisation (including the NGO/social sector organisation) to high levels of financial risk – on a daily basis. However, the complexity of the task in hand happens to be compounded many times over by that humongous fly-in-the-ointment called 'globalisation'.

For the NGO, operating in a closed environment/economy in a country can be taxing enough in terms of financial management. When that closed environment/economy is opened to the vagaries and far-reaching 'domino-esque' effects of globalisation, financial management becomes exponentially tougher. Financial management therefore poses a primary and sky-scraper high risk for the social sector organisation.

Financial risk is comprised of what I call a series of sub-risks. Smaller individual risks which together add up to the big one.

- - - - -

Finance Knowledge Risk (Skilled vs unskilled) – The first sub-risk in the Financial Risk realm, is the 'Finance knowledge risk' which is directly dependant on the presence of qualified, experienced finance people in the organisation and their skill-sets.

Simply put, would you set a fisherman to do a gold-smith's job or a carpenter to do a banker's job or vice versa? Nahin/Nein/Nyet/No – because the skill set or knowledge set each requires is vastly different from the other.

When it comes to managing financial risk, finance knowledge and knowing what to do in the realm of finance is half the battle won.

In the light of the complexities of the financial world, it is always wise to employ at least one (if not more) knowledgeable/skilled resource person to handle financial matters in the NGO. This resource should preferably be a Chartered Accountant or a Chartered Financial Analyst/PGDFA (ICFAI) or a Post Graduate in Management with a specialization in Finance. While the hiring and retaining of a qualified resource person is no doubt a slightly expensive proposition, for the mid to large size NGO, not hiring such a professional would prove to be an equally (if not more) expensive proposition, in the long run.

Why the above three qualifications, one might ask? Why not others? Simply because the obtention of either of these three qualifications entails a rigorous education in finance, accountancy, financial law, investments, etc. Finance, like most other disciplines, is based on a substantial body of theoretical knowledge – which can only be acquired through in-depth training and education by other people of similar skills/knowledge. People acquiring such qualifications have, literally, been put through the 'mill' and the ore has been converted into 'metal' - albeit of varying quality.

Simply put, the theoretical foundation for finance & financial management has been laid with people possessing such degrees. Knowledge has been acquired by them, which can be built upon with experience.

<u>Making do with semi-skilled or unskilled people to handle a critical area such as finance, can only result in the compounding of the risk arising out of lack of knowledge. A qualified, experienced finance manager can comprehend the complexities of finance, related law, statutory provisions & compliance, economic impacts, global movements, etc and hopefully devise plans to mitigate the risks arising out of the complexities.</u>

With a qualified resource person, financial risk is reduced in direct proportion to the person's ability to bring to bear their theoretical knowledge & experience, in steering the organisation out of financial difficulties or away from potential financial pitfalls.

<u>Disclaimer:</u> *The reduction, minimisation or mitigation of financial risk is NOT the result of the person's possession of either of the 3 degrees mentioned above but is solely dependant on their ability to utilize that which they have learnt during the acquisition of the degree – to positively impact the financial risk.*

For the smaller NGO, unable to afford such skilled yet costly manpower on a full-time basis, the solution is to hire such skills on contract basis or advisory basis – as part-time consultants or advisors.

The knowledge a skilled resource brings to the table will allow the organisation to tide over some of the below problem areas in Finance.

Bottomline: The organisation must have one reliable sheriff in town – the keeper of the financial law.

- - - - -

Cash & the NGO: Each and every NGO/social sector organisation operates with cash as a tool to get business done – no matter how small or large the ratio of cash transactions may be to the total. The very nature of our industry requires us to interact & deal with the less fortunate strata of society, the downtrodden, the poor, the underprivileged, etc. The majority of people, in this social strata, either do not have access to bank accounts or else have very low earnings which do not enable them to/permit them to adopt the banking habit. Their resultant preference in dealing in cash directly translates into the need for the NGO to transact in cash. The very presence of cash transactions introduces the cash risk factor into daily operations. This cash risk comes in many forms.

For our day-to-day use, how much cash do we need to hold as cash-in-hand? What is an optimal level of cash-in-hand? How frequently do we need to withdraw cash from our bank account/s? Who do we engage from our staff for carrying the cash after withdrawal from bank? What if the individual entrusted to make the cash withdrawal runs away with the organisation's cash? Where do we store the cash-in-hand? What if cash is stolen from our office? A multitude of questions arise when it comes to dealing with cash.

For any organisation high cash in hand comes with a cost. Too much cash in hand means that the excess cash could have been kept in the bank and earned interest or else could have been invested in a fixed deposit for a short or medium term and earned interest. Cash-in-hand is equal to idle money. Excessive cash-in-hand is bad financial management and carries with it the risks of loss of revenue and more importantly the risk of theft.

Very low cash in hand levels is just as bad and presents a different risk factor. It increases the need to make cash withdrawals from the bank to meet daily cash requirement, which in turn enhances the risk of theft of cash-in-transit. Not to mention the numerous trips to the bank which carry the cost of man-hours wasted as well as conveyance costs. Further, you will be faced with multiple instances in a year when at odd times & special days, you will require cash but the bank will be closed.

Cash therefore needs to be maintained at 'optimal levels' – not too high and not too low. So how do we ascertain this optimal level? Start by building a budget of your expenditures for the month, and the year. This should be based on past records/historical data. Break your monthly payments data into daily/weekly payment projections. Next forecast/estimate how much of your weekly payments are cash payments. The ratio of cash payments in a week to total payments will provide you with an Optimal Cash holding ratio (OCHR). This ratio may vary from month to month, based upon a project's cyclical nature or seasonal nature. An agri-based NGO may require higher cash levels in crop sowing season and harvest season and less during other months of the year. Once your optimal cash level has been forecasted add an extra 5–10% for contingencies. Ideally, your OCHR should help to reduce revenue loss, risk of theft, reduce cash withdrawal frequency, theft in transit, etc.

Even with the OCHR, the risk of theft of cash in transit from bank to office & vice-versa, does not get eliminated. Such risk cannot be eliminated but instead mitigated or reduced through insurance. Cash-in-transit & Cash in hand insurance policies pass on the risk of such theft, to the insurance – though for a fee called a premium. Risk of an employee (cashier) stealing cash can be covered with fidelity insurance.

- - - - -

Banking with risk: In our Indian scenario, banking seems to be one of the areas of difficulty to most people. My personal experience with banks has been one of mixed reactions. When interacting with a few public sector/nationalised banks, my experience has ranged from bordering on miserable to downright horrible – on account of attitude, delays in service, technologically-not-quite-there, etc. The private sector banks though operate in a different league altogether being technology-centric, much more customer friendly, process oriented, good ambience/branch décor, and so on. However, they too have their faults – their staff are quick to pounce on the unsuspecting account-holder to 'cross-sell' products that customers may not really need. Being a former private sector banker myself, there is no doubt where my vote goes when it comes to banking. Our public sector banks are presently undergoing a metamorphosis in an attempt to compete with their private sector counterparts, though they do have a long way to go to catch up.

Faced with the difficulties in service, attitude factor, etc is a factor which contributes less to an NGO's banking risk than the utter lack of knowledge about banking process or practice. Many of us just muddle through from day-to-day with regard to banking. Some people do not know how to write a cheque or fill out a deposit slip (whether to deposit cash or cheques). Strange, but true – the person may be qualified in the field of finance/accounts yet lacking the ability to write a cheque for the smallest of amounts or correctly fill in a deposit slip. Another basic knowledge gap on banking is knowing how to read a bank statement. One cannot properly operate a bank account of an NGO, without knowing the basic aspects of depositing money, withdrawing money, issuing cheques and reading bank account statements. Lack of knowledge on these very basic things puts the NGO squarely in the highest risk bracket when it comes to banking. Cheques can bounce for overwriting, inviting penal action from the drawee of the cheque (i.e. the beneficiary) or even worse, penalty (including arrest) in case of governmental/statutory dues such as Provident Fund or Employee State Insurance dues.

The advanced knowledge levels come next – Demand drafts & Pay Orders, clearing & CTS, money transfer mechanisms (RTGS, NEFT), KYC, FATCA, inward and outward remittances, IFSC codes, SWIFT & SWIFT codes, etc.

While the higher concepts of banking process are not expected of the layman or the average NGO manager, the greater the dependence on banking and bankers that the NGO has, the more important and inextricably intertwined these concepts become for the NGO. I will explain some of these concepts briefly and as simply as possible.

a. *Demand drafts/Pay orders:* This two items are something that many people confuse with each other, referring to Pay orders (PO) as Demand drafts (DD) and vice versa. A Pay order, as the name suggests is an order to a bank to pay to XYZ, and is payable in the SAME CITY as it is issued in. A Demand Draft is also an order to a bank to pay to XYZ, but payable in a DIFFERENT city than where it is issued. If you are based in Mumbai and want to make payment in Mumbai, you ask your bank for a Pay Order. If you want to make a payment in New Delhi, you ask your bank for a Demand Draft. Necessarily a demand draft cannot be paid in the city in which it is issued & a Pay Order cannot be paid in a city different from the city in which it is issued. One key feature of Demand drafts/Pay Orders is that both instruments have hard CASH backing them, because they are issued by your bank AFTER debiting your account. Therefore, for all practical purposes these instruments are CASH EQUIVALENT and cannot bounce.

b. *Clearing & CTS:* You receive a cheque from someone issued on X Bank. When you deposit that cheque with your bank (B Bank), your bank sends the cheque to X Bank (after encoding the cheque) to collect the money on your behalf. This is routed through the central bank/Apex bank of the country (Reserve Bank of India, in our country). This process of collecting the proceeds of cheques through a centralized system is called clearing. There are 2 basic types of clearing – local clearing (i.e. within the same city) and out-station clearing (inter-city clearing). Local clearing could take 2–3 days depending on your bank's rules while out-station clearing could take 3 days to 2 weeks.

CTS (Cheque Truncation System) is a rather recent technology brought in by Reserve Bank to cut short the clearing system timelines. With the older cheque clearing systems, physical instruments/cheques moved from each bank branch to RBI and from there to the cheque issuer's bank. The coordination and logistics were tremendous coupled with stringent timelines, which is why RBI introduced Cheque Truncation System, whereby your bank scans the cheque and sends the scans to the clearing house/ RBI which forwards it to the other bank. No physical instruments moving between banks – much faster, more efficient.

c. *Electronic Money transfer mechanisms:* In today's banking scenario, there are more advanced, efficient and quicker ways to send money. These methods are largely the 'online' methods or electronic transfer methods. First there is RTGS or Real Time Gross Settlement whereby funds are transferred through RBI's clearing systems on an online basis, without the need for a cheque to be issued to the beneficiary. RTGS is effected for amounts in excess of INR 200,000.

NEFT or National Electronic Funds Transfer is the same electronic funds transfer system, except that it is done for amounts above INR 1 (One Rupee).

IMPS or Immediate Payment Service – This allows you to transfer from Re. 1 to Rs. 200,000 at a time 365 days a year, 24×7.

In all of these cases, you need to have the receiver's bank details, account number and account name (accurate spelling as mentioned in the account).

You will also need the IFSC code of the beneficiary's bank.

d. *Cheque crossings:* When you issue a cheque to someone the issuance of the instrument carries with it an inherent risk. Surprised? You may issue a cheque to XYZ for Rs. 10000/-, without restricting the cheque for collection to just that person. If you take a look at your cheque-leaf, it says "Pay _____ or Bearer". The word 'bearer' means that should your cheque fall into the hands of the wrong person, that person becomes the de-facto 'bearer' and can encash it, resulting in financial loss to you or your organisation. Therefore, as a risk protection measure, we use various forms of 'crossings' on cheques. A 'crossing' is simply two parallel lines drawn close together on a cheque in the top-left hand corner or lower middle portion, which indicates to the bank that it is restricted to the beneficiary whose name is mentioned. Some crossed cheques can be endorsed to others by the named beneficiary. A common form of crossing used in the Indian banking system is that of the words 'A/c Payee' written between two parallel lines, meaning that the cheque is restricted to the bank Account of the beneficiary only.

Many NGOs are not familiar with the advanced payment processes or are apprehensive of using them, given the lack of familiarity with or distrust thereof. The result of not knowing & not using these advanced processes is the issuance of many cheques to make payment to vendors, beneficiaries, various parties, government, and others. This involves a lot of work writing cheques, handing them over to beneficiaries, tracking them till payment, doing the donkey work in case of cheque bounces (paying bounce charges, reissuing cheques), etc.

Cheques issued means you need to keep idle funds in your bank account, as you don't know when the beneficiary will deposit/present them in clearing. If on a particular day you have less funds in your bank account and any cheque issued hits in clearing, it will result in the cheque bouncing due to insufficient funds. Frequent occurrences will invite financial loss by way of cheque bounce charges and a bad credit reputation in the market. However, in addition to the risk of bad reputation and financial loss, is the financial risk of *notional revenue loss*. How so? The need to always maintain high balances in your account to avoid cheque bounces means that your money must lie idle in your bank earning very low returns/interest, when surplus money could be invested in a Term Deposit to earn your organisation some extra money.

Even with DDs/POs there is a finance risk – the risk of revenue loss. You see cash has already gone out from your account first when you request your banker to make a Demand Draft or Pay Order and has gone into the bank's pocket. When your beneficiary will deposit the DD/PO you do not know – it could be days or weeks later, which means the money locked in the DD/PO is not earning interest for you, resulting in notional revenue loss for your NGO.

Even if one knows these electronic payment terms & processes, the financial risk remains. It is wiser to adopt the online methods – for an NGO, pennies saved are pennies earned.

- - - - -

Foreign Exchange (Forex) risk – Many NGOs/social sector organisations are recipients of foreign funds for their operations and projects. Until the recent introduction of CSR (Corporate Social Responsibility), the funding gaps were largely bridged by donations from generous overseas donors/donor organisations, seeking to positively impact some aspect of social life in our country.

That very source of sustenance and financial viability for the NGO, believe it or not, presents an avenue of risk. Strange, is it not? How can your main pillar of support be the cause of concern? The risk present in the donations/overseas-grants, is the currency in which it is made. A donation/grant made in an overseas currency such as the US Dollar or Canadian Dollar or Euro or Singapore Dollar, carries with it the risk of currency fluctuation. We in India, transact in Indian

Rupees and every donation received in other currencies needs to be converted into our home currency which is the rupee.

Simply put, this rate of conversion is based on the price of a common basket of goods and services available from country to country. In simple terms, a basket of goods costs 1 US Dollar in USA and the same basket of goods may cost 60 Rupees in India. The foreign exchange rate therefore would be Rs. 60 per US Dollar.

Hypothetically speaking, this exchange rate should remain relatively stable over a period of time. Realistically, it changes minute to minute, second to second largely based on economic developments, perceptions, trade wars, speculation, et al.

That's the economics of it and the speculation of it. How does this impact you – the NGO manager/leader? How would the rupee's depreciation or appreciation against the US dollar or the Euro (or other foreign currency) impact your entity and its projects?

Let's take a simple example – let's say for one of your projects after much difficulty you have roped in an overseas donor to support you with a donation of US $ 10,000 over a year and your project cost is calculated at Rs. 650,000. The rupee/dollar exchange rate is Rs. 60/$. Your budget would look something like this, assuming that the exchange rate remains constant.

Scenario I

Sources	Rs.	Uses/costs	Rs.
$ 10,000 @ Rs. 60/$	600,000	Project expenses	650,000
Own contribution	50,000		
TOTAL	650,000	TOTAL	650,000

Scenario II

Since foreign exchange rates fluctuate from minute to minute, let's assume that at the beginning of the year, your donor sends you $ 3000 @ Rs. 60/$ and sends you another $ 3000 after 5 months @ Rs. 56/$

and the final instalment of $ 4000 after 9 months when the rate has become Rs. 62/$. Here's what your fund flows will look like, if your costs remain constant.

Sources	Rs.	Uses/costs	Rs.
$ 3,000 @ Rs. 60/$	180,000	Project expenses	650,000
$ 3,000 @ Rs. 56/$	168,000		
$ 4,000 @ Rs. 62/$	248,000		
Own contribution	54,000		
TOTAL	650,000	TOTAL	650,000

The financial risk arising out of the foreign exchange movement risk, in rupee terms, is Rs. 4000 additional burden by way of own contribution.

Scenario III

On the flip side, when the rupee depreciates by a good amount (say 10%), then the there is a gain to be had for the NGO.

Sources	Rs.	Uses/costs	Rs.
$ 3,000 @ Rs. 60/$	180,000	Project expenses	650,000
$ 3,000 @ Rs. 63/$	189,000		
$ 4,000 @ Rs. 66/$	264,000		
Own contribution	17,000		
TOTAL	650,000	TOTAL	650,000

The financial risk arising out of the foreign exchange movement risk, in rupee terms, is Rs. 33000 gain by way of the own contribution portion being reduced by a large amount due to forex conversion gain.

The foreign exchange risk determines whether your project becomes cash surplus or cash deficit, at the end of the day/project duration. This in turn directly translates into a financing nightmare or a bonanza.

The tragic part of the story is neither of us have control on the movement of foreign currency exchange rates, and therefore must resort to risk mitigation strategies.

One trick each NGO manager should be aware of is the concept of 'Card rates' versus 'Inter Bank Rates' for foreign exchange. All banks offer you a standard rate for the day when you are selling dollars (i.e. you have received dollars and are selling to the bank to get rupees) or vice versa when you are buying dollars. This standard rate is called the 'card rate' and is based on yesterday's closing exchange rate for the dollar/other currency. The 'inter-bank rate' is the dynamic rate for today, at which the bank buys and sells dollars in the foreign currency market today. It is the most current rate available. Know this – the bank will not offer you the inter-bank rate from the get-go. Reason – the bank's profit comes from buying/selling in the inter-bank market at the inter-bank rates and selling/buying with you at the card rates. It's an arbitrage game wherein the bank pockets the difference in the two rates – and the bank never loses.

The net result for you as an NGO Finance manager is that the exchange rate today may be Rs. 62.5/$ in the inter-bank market, but you may get a rate of Rs. 61/$ on the card rate. A rate of even Rs. 62/$ would mean a gain of Rs. 10000 on a donation/grant of $ 10000.

As NGOs, we are not permitted to enter into hedging instruments such as forward contracts, forex futures, forex swaps, etc as these are deemed speculative instruments and speculative instruments are prohibited under the FCRA Act.

However, if you are the recipient of a large sum of foreign currency each year, you can negotiate with your banker to provide you rates based on the daily inter-bank foreign exchange rate. Necessarily, no banker worth his salt would offer you the inter-bank rate (IBR) but instead would give you IBR plus some margin as a rate offer. Better realisations = better finance = less forex risk.

- - - - -

To budget or not to budget risk – In a recent seminar/finance-overview-cum-training I conducted, I was quite stunned to discover that less than 10% of my target audience actually knew what a budget or budgeting was, let alone know how to make a rudimentary budget. Similarly, can one initiate a Rs. 5 crores (i.e. Rs. 50 million) project minus a budget?

For a hardcore Finance-man, this is an unthinkable crime, even by the uninitiated. At any point of time, when it comes to dealing with money – even for one's own household – it is absolutely imperative that you build a budget. For the financially uninitiated, what is a budget? A budget is simply a statement of estimates of your uses of funds and sources of funds for a particular project or period. It shows you whether, at the end of the period/project, you have funds left over or need extra funds to cover the estimated expenditure.

Well, at this juncture, you may ask – what's so great or earth-shattering about a budget and where is the risk factor in a budget? The reality of budgeting is – without a budget you will never know at the start of a project or time period what your possible end-scenario for funds is likely to be. If you start a project without projecting or estimating your financial outflows & inflows, you will end up with a small, medium or whopping deficit at the end of the period, with no means to take corrective action whatsoever. When the books are finally written, it will be time to sell the family silver/gold to make good the deficit on a project of your NGO.

Many of us tend to think that because our organisation receives a few thousand rupees (or a few lakhs), we don't need to budget. Whether a few thousands, a few hundred thousand or a few millions, a budget can be one of the best pals when dealing with money.

The risk aspect in budgeting is in not budgeting at all or not acting on an adverse budget. The purpose of a budget is manifold.

i. It helps to estimate/forecast expenditure and incomes for a project or a time period.

ii. It helps to estimate/forecast the end surplus or deficit for a project or a time period.

iii. If built on a monthly fund flow budget pattern, it can help to ascertain which months have higher expenditure (i.e. busy months) and arrange/provide funds to match the busy month's money requirement. As a result, there will be little or no fund flow mismatch.

iv. It helps one plan the organisation's investments better, to obtain best returns. For example, if your donor provides your funds upfront, while expenditure is over a period of time, you can invest the funds in fixed deposits to mature in a staggered manner, so as to match your project outflows. In the bargain, you earn interest which can help to reduce your possible deficit or ensure you end with a surplus.

v. It enables one to develop an ACTION PLAN, in case of deficits. If you wait for the books to be written and then find a deficit, all you can do is wring your hands and sell the family silver to make up the deficit. With a budget deficit, you can draw up a multi-point action plan to reduce/nullify the deficit from the get-go and start work on the plan.

The Action Plan bit is the risk mitigator in your budget pack. If you do not budget, you will not know where you stand. It will be like a blind man taking a walk down the labyrinth – a rather painful and risky exercise, let me assure you. If you budget and find a deficit and do nothing, that's like negotiating a mine-field in the daytime with your eyes closed.

There is financial risk in every business/money-related venture. The budget helps to identify some of the risks and point you towards the risk-mitigator called the action plan.

- - - - -

These are just some of the many financial risks we face on day-to-day basis as managers and leaders of NGOs. The list gets longer and more complex as we expand in value and diversity of our projects. Financial risk is threat factor we can ill afford to ignore or not assess and if assessed, fail to take action on.

Most of us know the story of the Apostle Peter and his denial of the Christ after which the cock crowed three times.

For many of us in our NGOs, for our denial of the financial risk the cock will not crow thrice – the first time itself will spell disaster.

Chapter IV

Operational & Procedural Risk

"In the land of the blind, the one-eyed man is king!"

– Desiderius Erasmus

Allow me to begin this chapter with what I call the 'Theory of Chaos'. This nomenclature, of course, has no basis in scientific theory nor is it in relation to the 'Chaos theory' which is an altogether complex branch of mathematics.

The name merely lends itself to the description of a scenario which many NGOs find themselves in post formation/establishment and a scenario which a good number still continue to find themselves in, despite being operational for a number of years. Such situations could owe themselves to the lack of clarity in the minds of founding members at the time of formation/registration of the NGO, while for those entities already functional for a number of years, such prevailing situations could only be attributable to the sheer ignorance of the need to bring order where there is chaos.

Chaos, typically, is the lack or absence of order. Chaos once spawned begets chaos which in turn begets more chaos, until someone – with an eye for process – comes along and takes a very sharp axe to the chaos tree.

The seeds of chaos are often sown rather unwittingly once the organisation is formed or even before it is formed. The well-meaning, uninitiated founder sees a need in society and sets up an entity to cater to the need. In many cases, this is where the seed of chaos gets sown. Merely identifying a need in society, contemplating and establishing the vehicle (type of NGO) to meet that need, does not result in the need being meet or even adequately catered to. Even if the NGO starts functioning, the social need may not get met on account of disjointed functionality.

Sadly, yours truly has been witness to an NGO operating for decades in the absence of well-defined, well-adhered-to process. In some cases, there may be no organizational hierarchy to manage things as well as no clearly documented procedures. Things are interpreted and procedures determined from day-to-day, hour-to-hour. What happens in an organisation where there is no process orientation or where there is no decentralization of authority – a sort of one-man show – "I am all in all". More scary – what if there is no accountability? The individual leader is accountable to no-one. We are all familiar with the saying – "Power corrupts and absolute power corrupts absolutely".

The result can be described in a word – 'Chaos'!

Anyone familiar with the story of creation will nod their heads at the similarity between such a scenario and the situation described in the book of Genesis (in the Bible) chapter 1 verse 2: "The earth was without form and void; and darkness was on the face of the deep. ..."

What, therefore, does it take for us to bring "light to this darkness" and "shape and structure to this void" – to this formless chaos?

To achieve this, one must flex the 'muscles' of one's grey matter and embark on a thoughtful journey of contemplation and analysis coupled with a healthy dose of common sense. Let's hit that road to bring structure and clarity to the chaos.

Let us begin with the simple question "WHAT"?

What will my NGO do – what kind of activity and what kind of social need will it fulfil? For an existing NGO, you need to ask – what kind of activity does my entity do and what kind of social need does it fulfil?

The NGO/not-for-profit entity (new or existing) may be a religion based one (i.e. church, temple, mosque, gurdwara, etc) or social need based one or human rights based one or even a political one. Then ascertain the kind of need the NGO will fulfil. Some NGOs are 'singular-activity' organisations – they focus on one kind of activity alone (e.g. charity clinics, dispensaries, education, skill training, etc). Then there are the others, which are 'multi-activity' organisations – they focus on more than one kind of activity alone (e.g. some religious organisations with schools/children's homes, hospitals with medical colleges, etc). Each of these activities should be found in the organisation's Memorandum of Association/Trust Deed/founding document in what is known as the 'Objects clause' or else as part of the 'other/ancillary objectives'.

Once these core activities are listed, we must proceed to use these as the building blocks of a 'functional activity ORG chart' for the organisation. What is an 'org chart'? For those unaware, an org chart means an 'organisation chart', wherein the functioning units/departments of an organisation are shown in a graphical form. In this case, it's a mapping or graphical representation of the NGO's activity/activities.

With the activities listed, let us assume that the fulfilment of each activity needs processes or departments. Let us refer to each activity as a 'vertical' and any subsidiary activity/department as a 'sub-vertical'. To provide a clearer understanding of this, let us take a couple of examples.

Example 1 – Let us assume that there is a church (you can substitute this with any other religious entity according to your personal preference) which has different language groups which meet for worship on Sundays/other days as well as other church-based activities. It also has schools for imparting education (full-paying and free schools), vocational skills training, theological training, a hospital, a children's-education-sponsorship programmes, and a social outreach/benevolence programmes for the poor, etc.

In this example, the verticals would be as follows:

a. Church congregations vertical

b. Education vertical

c. Hospital & healthcare vertical

d. Education sponsorship vertical

e. Social Benevolence vertical

When considering sub-verticals, this list could get expanded as follows.

a. Church congregations vertical
   i. Language congregation 1
   ii. Language congregation 2
   iii. Language congregation 3
   iv. Other church-based activities
   v. Theological training

b. Education vertical
   i. Full paying schools
   ii. Free schools
   iii. Skill training schools
   iv. College

c. Hospital & healthcare vertical
   i. Hospital (full paying including clinics/dispensaries)
   ii. Free clinics

d. Education sponsorship vertical

e. Social Benevolence vertical
   i. Healthcare for poor
   ii. Soup-kitchens/feeding programmes
   iii. Children's home (for orphans and poor children)
   iv. Substance abuse rehab programmes (including hospitalization)

Now let's take a look at another example – that of a hospital with medical colleges and satellite clinics/hospitals. The verticals and sub-verticals could appear as follows.

a. Hospital & Healthcare (full paying)

    i. Neurosurgery department

    ii. Cardiology department

    iii. Endocrinology department

    iv. Obstetrics & Gynaecology department

    v. Haematology department

    vi. Paediatrics department

    vii. Radiology department, etc

    viii. Out-patient clinics (paying)

    ix. Satellite Hospitals

    x. Pharmacy, etc

b. Medical education/colleges

    i. Medical college

    ii. Dental college

    iii. Nursing school/college,

    iv. Student hostels, etc

c. Healthcare Benevolence

    i. Free clinics

    ii. Free substance abuse & rehab

    iii. Poor patients' treatment programmes

d. Clinical trials

In a similar manner, if we scrutinize each sub-vertical, we will find 'micro-verticals' under the sub-verticals. For example, in the 2nd illustration, there may be four or five hostels for the college students. Or there may a 'Bone-Marrow-transplant' setup in the Haematology section.

In Illustration 1, there may be a micro vertical of a summer camp or a Christmas programme under the 'other church-based activities' sub-vertical.

There is no limit to the number of verticals/sub-verticals/micro-verticals an NGO can have. However, the more is NOT the merrier. Remember, the more you stretch elastic the thinner it becomes. Having too many verticals makes an NGO a lumbering beast – massive, slow and ungainly and quite possibly inefficient too.

The hidden verticals – Every NGO has at least one hidden vertical, which it needs to provide for in the functional activity org chart. This is known as the 'administration' vertical. Without administration, no organisation can function irrespective of whether it is a one-vertical business or a multi-vertical business. The administration vertical would generally have three sub-verticals of (a) Human Resources (staff), (b) Finance and (c) General Admin. These have been slotted under one separate vertical to bring unity of control & unity of focus to each component, instead of repeating these items under each department/sub-vertical. It also helps to limit the number of micro-verticals in the activity org chart.

Now let us proceed to give diagrammatical shape to these two examples. (See diagram 1: Functional Activity Org Chart with verticals, sub-verticals & micro verticals (example 1) & Diagram 2: Functional Activity Org Chart with verticals, sub-verticals & micro verticals (example 2))

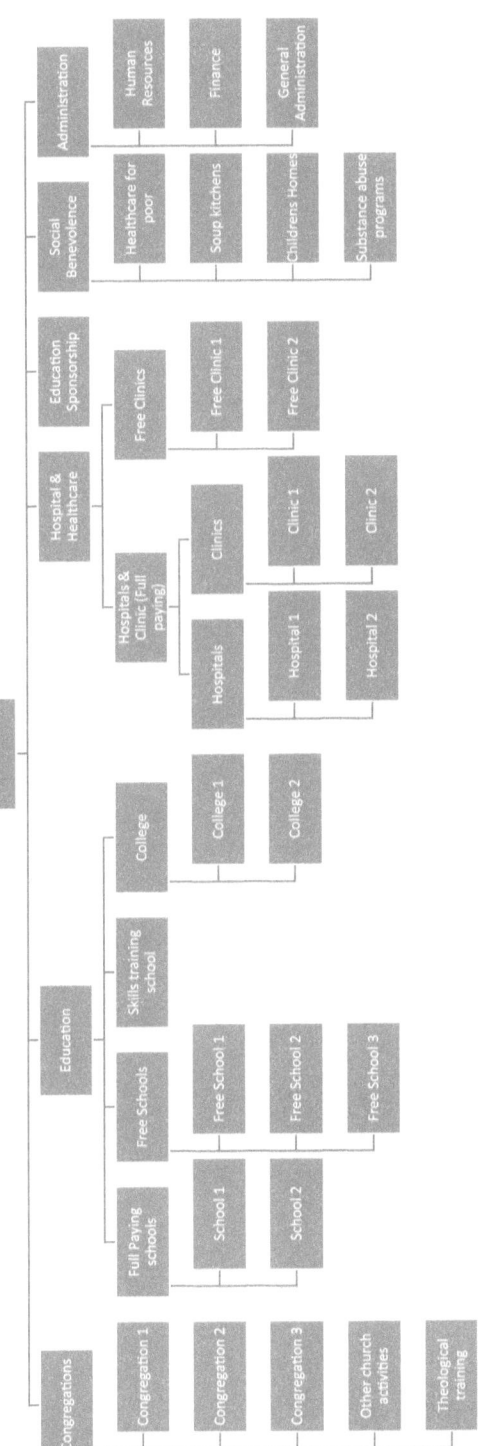

Diagram 1: Functional Activity Org Chart with verticals, sub-verticals & micro verticals (example 1)

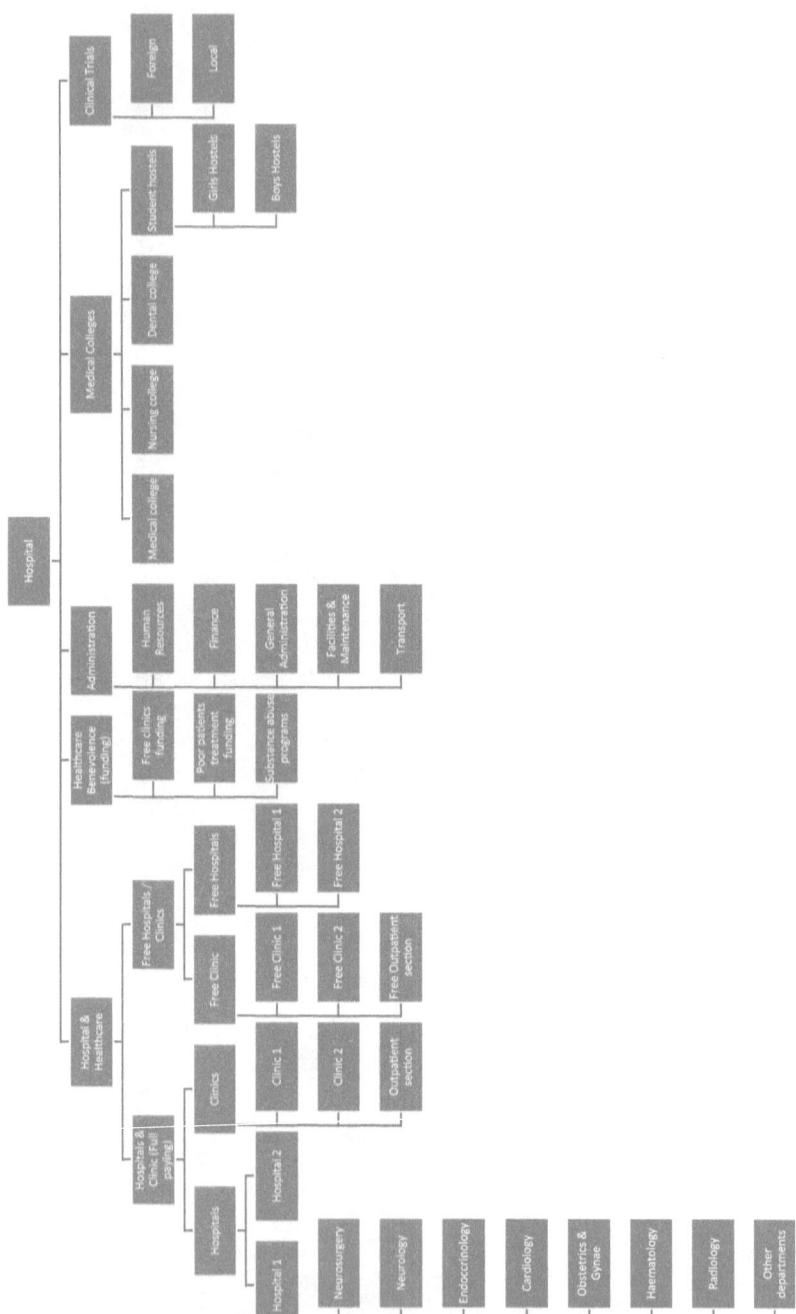

Diagram 2: Functional Activity Org Chart with verticals, sub-verticals & micro verticals (example 2)

Having completed the functional activity org chart, let us proceed to the next step – the process org chart. This org chart will cover the various activities that the administration vertical of the organisation shall carry out. Do not mistake these processes for functional activities. Some of these processes are: Purchases of non-asset items/sales/recruitment of staff at various levels/investments/purchase of assets/budgeting/staff administration, etc. There may be other processes not mentioned here, which may be unique to your organisation. Go right ahead and include them. Next, map all these processes in a similar manner as with the functional activity org chart. (see Diagram 3 – Process Org Chart)

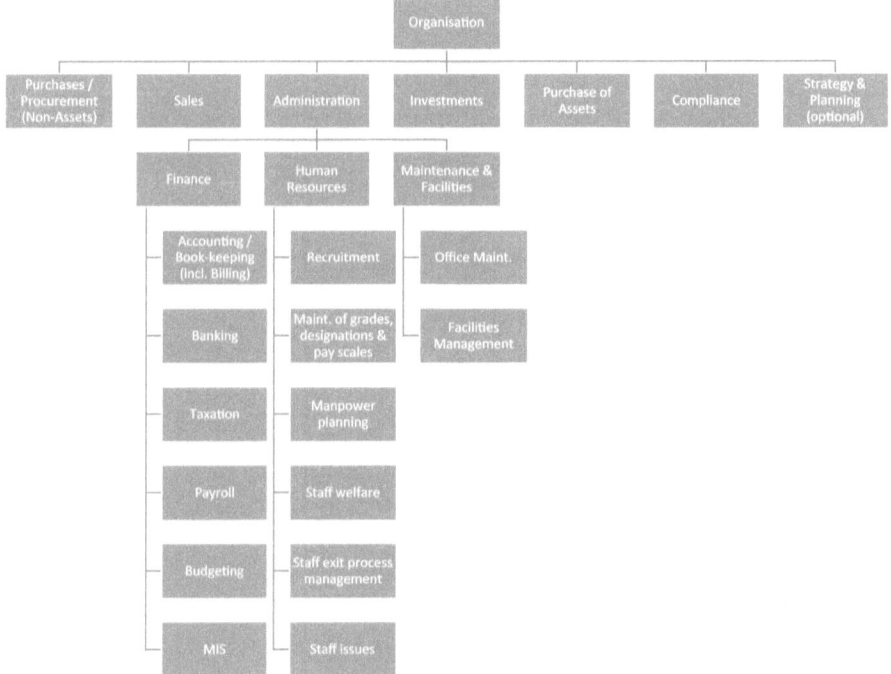

Diagram 3: Process Org Chart

Next, let us proceed to the final org chart which is the employee org chart, wherein the employees of your organisation must be reflected in a hierarchical manner based on their designations. (In reality this would represent the 'pecking order'). This is an extremely extensive exercise as you will need to do this for each sub-vertical and micro-vertical.

For example, under the Administration vertical & Finance sub-vertical - your Accounts & Finance department may comprise of Helper/clerk/peon, Trainee Accountant, Junior Accountant, Accountant, Senior Accountant, Accounts Officer, Deputy Accounts Manager, Accounts Manager, Senior Accounts Manager, Chief Accounts Manager, Director – Finance & Accounts. For a new organisation, you will need to plan for/decide on how many designation levels you would like to have (or would need) in your organisation. Try and keep this to the bare minimum.

Similarly, a Purchases department could consist of Trainee, Junior Purchase Assistant, Purchase Assistant, Purchases Officer, Dy. Purchase Manager, Purchases Manager, etc.

For a school, it could be it could be Helper, Trainee Teacher, Assistant Teacher, Teacher, Sectional Head (Junior/Senior school), Vice Principal, Headmaster/Headmistress/Principal, etc.

For a hospital sub-vertical, Helper, Attendant/Ward Boy, Trainee Nurse, Assistant Nurse, Nurse, Nurse (Grade I/Grade II,), Doctor (various categories upto department head), etc.

Necessarily in this hierarchical chart you will also need to factor in the place for the organisation head (Chairman/Director/CEO, etc) as well as the apex accountability body (Board/Governing body, etc). (see Diagram 4: Employee/Staff (Hierarchical) Org chart)

Having completed this seemingly long-drawn exercise, let us now proceed to the crux of the matter – deciding the operational & procedural aspects. First, spread all 3 org charts on the table and begin with processes which are common across the organisation. Let's take purchases as an example. For a process such as purchase of regular items (non-assets) we need to look at the following.

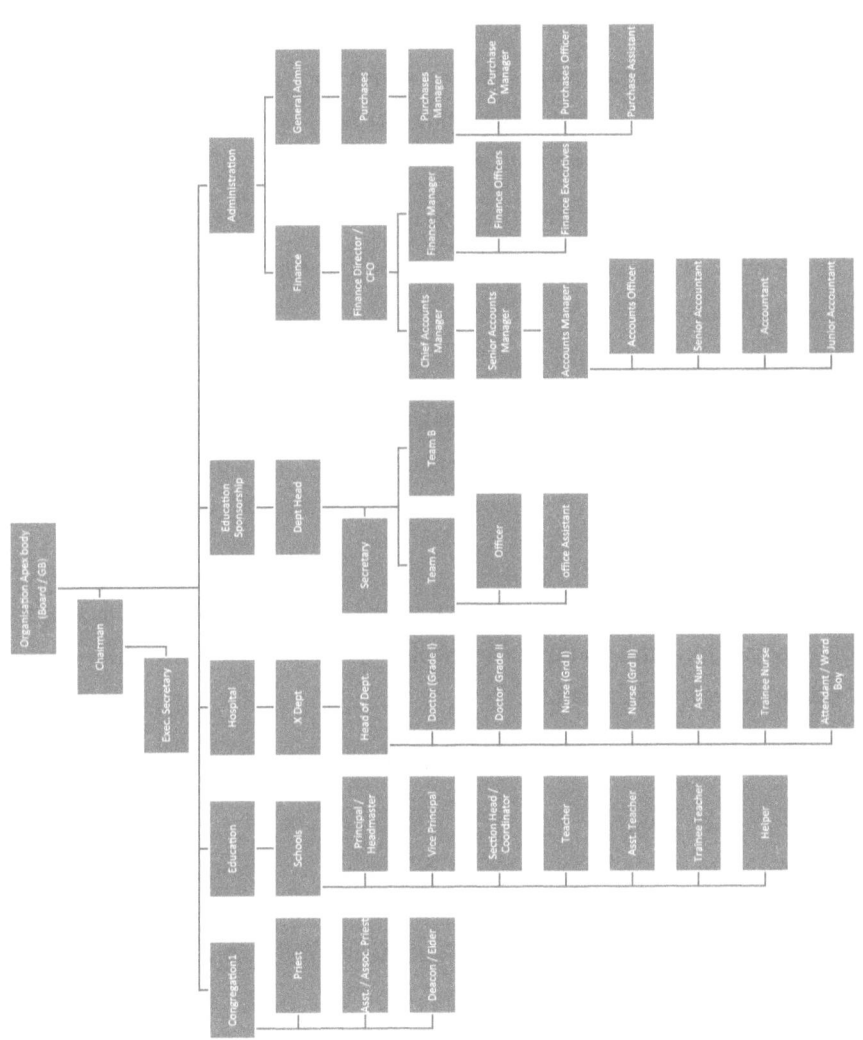

Diagram 4: Employee/Staff (Hierarchical) Org chart

a. What are the common items purchased/to be purchased on regular basis?

b. What would be the approximate quantum (number & value) per month/per week?

c. Who should be responsible for such purchases?

d. Will the person/people in (c) above be conferred with approval powers? If so, how much in value terms? If not, then who would have approval powers and upto what limit?

e. How will purchase orders be placed – written or verbal?

f. How will the purchase order be tracked for fulfilment (quantity & quality)?

g. Any other relevant aspects.

Similarly, a set of question/aspects need to be arrived at for recruitment of staff, administration of personnel, investments, sales, asset purchase, etc. Make a list of the operational & procedural aspects which need to be looked into/answered.

(In some cases, it may be wise to make the list of procedural aspects first before defining the hierarchical employee org chart, as it can impact the definition/structure of the latter).

Now let us start building our operational guidelines and delegation of powers.

Delegation of powers: The delegation of powers in any organisation can be spread across many levels or restricted to just a few people or even a single individual – depending on the level of decentralisation the apex body/founder chooses. A centralised approval structure allows for financial/non-financial approval powers to be vested in the hands of only one or at best just a few. The decentralised approach spreads the approval powers across some layers of the staff org chart. Let us look at a simple illustration-cum-comparison for both approaches for the Purchases illustration (relevant parts) provided before.

Table 1: Centralised vs Decentralised approach

	Centralised approach	Decentralised approach
a. What would be the approximate quantum (number & value) per month/per week? INR 500,000 per month INR 125,000 per week		
b. Who should be responsible for such purchases? INR 500,000 per month INR 125,000 per week	Director Director	Purchases Manager/CFO/Director Purchases Manager/CFO/Director
c. Will the person/people in (b) above be conferred with approval powers? If so, how much in value terms? If not, then who would have approval powers and upto what limit?	Director (unlimited powers)	Upto INR 30000 per week – Purchases Manager INR 30000 to INR 90000 per week – Director or CFO Above INR 90000 per week – Director

It is essential to note that there are pros and cons with both styles. If you employ a largely centralised approach wherein powers are not delegated but centralised in one person there is a high level of control on decisions. Among the cons, however, it implies that the one-downs are not capable/qualified to take decisions (financial or non-financial) or it could also imply that the one-downs are not trustworthy. Also, the organisation may find itself in a tight spot where urgent purchases may be needed but the one authorised person to approve is out-station/out of the country on important business. Or worst-case scenario, what if the individual authorised misuses his powers to demand kick-backs for every approval?

I am aware of an organisation wherein the centralisation of powers in one man's hands turned the man into a self-styled dictator, which left the organisation dealing with legacy issues directly resulting from his 'one-man's-wisdom' approach.

The positives of the decentralised approach include avoidance of a 'no-approver-available' situation and a greater sense of responsibility & accountability among the one-downs. It also negates the 'dictator' style leadership phenomenon. However, the decentralised system necessitates a greater level of checks and balances to prevent the abuse of approval powers.

If your organisation's apex body wishes to go ahead with a centralised approach to all things, then operational/procedural guidelines are a no-brainer really. Every decision rests with one man and one man alone.

However, if the decision is to go 'decentralised', then you need to put the brain cells to the task. For this management style, not only is a delegation of powers necessary, it is also vital to develop operational/procedural guidelines also known as 'Standard Operating Procedures' or SOPs.

The method to working out a judicious delegation of powers and SOPs is as follows.

Step 1:   Look first at the process chart you have developed, selecting one process at a time.

Step 2:   Next look at the Functional Activity Org chart and ask the question – is it a process which is common to all the verticals/sub-verticals? If yes, then we devise a common delegation of powers for the process.

Step 3:   Look at the set of questions you have listed for this particular process.

Step 4:   Answer the questions one by one, while keeping in front of you the Employee Org chart. When you come to a process question about allocating responsibility or authority, look at the employee org chart and decide which level of person should be vested with what type of responsibility or authority. Responsibility can be shared among various levels of people and so can authority. At the same time, process responsibility can be shared among many while process authority restricted to a few.

Step 5:   Write down the responsibility/authority, lest you forget. It is advisable to put the results into a table/matrix/grid-form, similar to Table 2 below.

Follow this logic for all the common processes to work out the responsibility/authority levels.

There may be other questions on the questions list which are not employee related, such as:

a.   What are the common items purchased/to be purchased on regular basis?

b.   What would be the approximate quantum (number & value) per month/per week?

c.   How will purchase orders be placed – written or verbal?

d.   How will the purchase order be tracked for fulfilment (quantity & quality)?

Answer these questions also, filling in the answers in the procedure column (see Table 2 below).

Table 2: Procedure/Responsibility/Authority matrix

Process = Purchases (common)	Procedure	Responsibility	Authority
a. What would be the approximate quantum (number & value) per month/ per week?	INR 500,000 per month INR 125,000 per week		

Continued…

b.	Who should be responsible for such purchases? INR 500,000 per month INR 125,000 per week		Dy. Purchase Manager & Purchase Manager	
c.	Will the person/ people in (b) above be conferred with approval powers? If so, how much in value terms? If not, then who would have approval powers and upto what limit?	Approval needed from Apex body		Upto INR 30000 per week – Purchases Manager INR 30000 to INR 90000 per week – Director or CFO Above INR 90000 per week – Director
d.	How will purchase orders be placed – written or verbal?	May be placed verbally, followed by written Purchase order to vendor, signed by person/persons authorised under the DOP		
e.	How will the purchase order be tracked for fulfilment (quantity & quality)?	i. Quantity to be checked (by 2 purchases staff) against purchase order, on delivery ii. Quality of goods to be verified by Stores dept., or by Utilising dept.		

In the steps listed above, we dealt with a process that is common across verticals and hence we evolved a common procedure/responsibility/authority matrix. What if a process is not common across the organisation but is specific to a particular vertical/sub-vertical? Let's go back to Step 2 for this.

Step 2A: Next look at the Functional Activity Org chart and ask the question – is it a process which is common to all the verticals/sub-verticals? For a non-common process, we need to devise a separate delegation of powers & SOPs for that process, specific to that vertical.

Let us assume that one department/sub-vertical of your organisation has a recurring requirement for highly specialised but items, which cannot be ordered through a common process, nor its quality be verified by purchases dept. In such cases, you will need a separate Delegation of Powers & SOP, different from the common process one.

Step 3: List a separate set of questions you have listed for this particular process.

Step 4: Answer the questions one by one, while keeping in front of you the Employee Org chart. When you come to a process question about allocating responsibility or authority, look at ONLY the portion of the employee org chart which pertains to that sub-vertical/department, and decide which level of person there should be vested with what type of responsibility or authority. (Example: specialised DVDs for every-day use could be authorised/approved by an IT Systems manager)

Step 5: Write down the responsibility/authority, lest you forget. It is advisable to put the results into a table/matrix/grid-form, similar to Table 2.

Deviations: Every good Delegation of powers & SOPs, should contain a deviations matrix. A deviations matrix is simply a statement of who is authorised to do what or is responsible for what in contingency situations. For example, let us say the Director in Table 2 above is on a week's leave/hospitalised or whatever, and an urgent purchase for INR 125000 needs to be approved. The deviations matrix could provide for joint approval by Purchase Manager & CFO, in such a situation, with due ratification by the Director on his return.

Now that you have your procedural guidelines (SOPs) and delegation of powers in written/matrix form, the final step is to convert it into a written document or manual for use across the organisation. Based on this manual, you can further develop detailed job roles for employees at various levels in the organisation. The procedure manual/SOPs and job-roles then become the basis for operational control, performance appraisal & even disciplinary action (in case procedures are not followed/violated at any time).

I have provided below an extract from a sample Delegation of Powers, for you to understand how you can build your procedure manual.

Sample Delegation of Powers (DOP)

1. Upto Rs. 50000/- per item per instance (Secretary/Treasurer individually)

2. Greater than Rs. 50000 & Upto Rs. 75000 per item per instance (Secy. & Treasurer jointly).

3. Greater than Rs. 75000 & Upto Rs. 100,000 per item per instance – Chairman jointly with Secy./treasurer.

4. Above Rs. 100000, Apex Body to approve.

5. The above DOP to remain in force for 1 year from the date of adoption by the Apex Body. After 1 year, the DOP may be reviewed and revised by the Apex Body, based on ground realities.

- - - - -

Changes to SOPs: With the passage of time, some procedures become redundant and need replacement by new ones or procedure modifications. What should be the prescribed course of action here? Should we scrap the old manual and build a new one? To answer this, I must draw on my experience as an ex-banker. Banks adopt a methodology of having a process manual for different products/departments. Procedural changes are issued through 'circulars' or official memos/documents which refer to and detail the changes to procedures mentioned in 'X' circular of so-and-so date.

The circular issued must then be appended to the operations manual for future reference.

I have personally used the issuance of circulars to good effect – whether to prescribe a new process, modify an existing one and even formalize/document an existing verbal process.

Now that we have established a reasonable level of clarity by defining procedures as well as the guidelines for almost every process, compare the then with the now. The absence of procedural & operational guidelines presents the organisation with the prospect of very severe risk. Listing the risks that can occur in the absence of operational guidelines, is beyond the scope of this chapter.

Operational & procedural risk is like walking eyes
closed through a minefield.

Chapter V

Donor Risk

The times they are a-changing! As I mentioned before, we live and operate in a dynamic environment. Gone are the days of the 80s and 90s when funds were relatively easy to come by in comparison to the current day scenario. I know of the founder of an NGO who could mobilise funds for his organisation's projects with a few telephone calls overseas.

It was then that donors (mostly overseas) funded philanthropic projects based on a tug of the heart strings. Emotions ruled mostly, when it came to decisions to support a project or a church or an ashram and so on. Emotions do still play a part in funding decisions today but the overarching factors that govern donors' decisions today are economics, finance and results.

Consequently, no donor relationship is a guarantee against the passage of time anymore. In our dynamic world environment today, the very source of the NGO's support has also become one of its biggest risks.

In chapter II of this book, I had briefly touched upon how this is probably one of the areas of greatest concern for an NGO – because donors constitute among the highest degrees of risk to any non-profit organisation. We never seem to consider that the funding tap can be turned off at the drop of a hat or the turn of a whim.

Human psychology dictates that when you are higher up in the pecking order or at the top of it, lesser mortals display a greater tendency to dictate terms and a strong tendency to 'blow with the wind'. The same applies when you are the one putting down the money for a charitable cause. The tendency is to lord it over the donee (i.e. the NGO) or move the funds to some other avenue at a perceived slight or perceived deficit in delivery or goal fulfilment. This psychological factor places a heavy burden of responsibility (though often unspoken) on the donee. It is a risk based on human character – the whip called bargaining power. A risk I prefer to term as 'flight risk'.

Donor conversion ratio is low – Post the Wall Street crisis of 2008, many banks folded up taking with them many of their High Net Worth (HNW) clients and causing many an economy to flounder, the world over. The resultant effect is that many social sector funding organisations in the USA & Europe felt a severe pinch from declining philanthropic contributions/donations. The belt-tightening began overseas and the breathlessness and suffocation began to be felt by NGOs in India. Donors facing wage cuts or job losses, who had previously donated for education, healthcare, general operations; now cut back on all except donating for education of poor children or stopped donating altogether.

The donor pie became smaller overnight, jacking up the ratio of funding proposals to actual commitments. The same donors now receive proposals from several hundreds of NGOs a year, as compared to a hundred or a couple of hundred before. The ratio of hits to misses has declined substantially, posing NGOs with the increased risk of proposal rejections by donors/agencies.

Non-compliance – Many of us are under the mistaken assumption that a donor needs to donate his or her money to our project and forget about it. We believe that this is the limit of the donor's authority/ scope/role. We tend to not consider that a donor might have rules and laws to comply with in his or her own country or even in India. For example, a donation to a Trust registered under 80G of the Income Tax Act 1961 mandates that we issue an 80G marked receipt to the donor, for tax benefit purposes. Non-issuance of the receipt renders the donor ineligible to claim the tax benefit at the time of filing Income Tax returns.

In a similar manner, overseas donors might require certain documentation standards to be complied with by us in order for them to fulfil their tax/legal compliance in their home country. I know of one such overseas donor which requires an acknowledgement of receipt of funds to be issued by the donee, in which 3 persons must sign off and none of the 3 can be related to each other by blood. Prima facie it may sound strange, but legally it negates or minimises the scope of collusion for fraud. Similarly, an overseas donor might require documentary submissions as proof of spending/expenditure or even quotations before release of funds for purchase of equipment/ assets. Do not be alarmed, it may be a compliance requirement for adhering to the internal revenue service laws of the donor's country.

When we hesitate/refuse to ascertain or even comply with a donor's documentation standards, we are directly subjecting ourselves to the donor cancellation risk or donor exit risk, as no donor will be willing to face government/revenue service penalties arising out of documentary non-compliance by a donee. It could result in the cancellation of licences, permissions and even closure of the donor's organisation. This risk for the donor is too high to bear for the sake of an NGO that cannot comprehend documentary compliance or adhere to it.

Our non-compliance is the quintessential boomerang, which comes back to hit us in the wrong place. When we don't comply with what the donor needs, the resultant effect is that the donor will not comply with what we need – i.e. funds. This is the consequence of the non-compliance risk.

MIS Risk – A continuation of paragraph 1 of this chapter is the MIS Risk or Management Information System Risk (MISR) – which in a lighter vein can prove to be quite a 'MIS-ery' for the average NGO. Donors will no longer sit on the side-lines anymore, instead they will take an active part in the projects we ask them to fund. They are now accountability oriented and MIS focussed. One aspect of their active participation is the asking for of MIS or progress reports on the project/s they fund. A simple MIS would be to show the amount of money spent from the money sent by the donor, the amount left and how each expense reflects against the budget presented before the start of the project.

More detailed MIS would take the form of progress reports on the 'achievables' or end-result parameters which measure the results the project was actually supposed to achieve. These may be detailed field reports, base-line surveys of beneficiaries, impact assessment studies, etc.

These kinds of MIS, however, are not the MIS Risk. One form of MIS Risk is the absence of a system or methodology to develop/ generate such MIS for the donor is the actual risk. There must be a process/method set in place, at the time of starting a project, whereby it is a relatively simple matter to extract (or mine) the data required and to present it in proper format to the donor.

A second form of donor risk is when the donor already has a format for submitting reports/information and the NGO lacks the expertise/personnel to understand/interpret the format and provide the data accurately in the donor's format.

Bargaining power risk – This is one aspect to donors that all of us hate the most – the bargaining power of a donor. All of us know what bargaining power is – the bigger your customer/donor, the greater can be the (unreasonable!) demands. Such donors present us with a huge bargaining power risk. As the recipients of their support funds, we cannot afford to antagonize them in order to avoid them pulling the plug – hence we can't be too 'strict'. Neither can we be too lax and allow them to ride rough-shod over us. This risk results in us walking a very difficult tightrope for the sake of our projects.

- - - - -

Mitigating Donor Risk

How do we go about managing this very critical risk area? In order to mitigate donor risk, it is essential that we ensure a few basic steps/precautions before engaging a donor to support our projects.

> ➤ Draw the broad contours of the relationship before the money starts coming in. These contours will in turn become the boundary walls for your relationship with the donor. *Do not forget to quote the relevant portions of law which dictate your limitations as far as dealing with your donor is concerned.* In the same manner as your donor is accountable to his/her authorities in their home country, they must know your accountability level before the authorities in your own country. There are certain things that we are not allowed to do. For example, for foreign donations we cannot be seen to be functioning as an 'agent' of the foreign body/donor – which is what would happen if the donor dictates terms to us.

> ➤ Understand the donors regulatory/compliance requirements in his/ her home country, in terms of taxation, registration, special rules relating to overseas donations/charity, etc. All of this knowledge will help you to understand why the donor asks for a certain documentation standard, certain types of reports, etc. Knowing their legal and statutory requirements help you to help them better. This will help to mitigate the compliance risk.

> ➤ Get to know the donor's timelines & quantifiables for the project. Understand the types of reports they need and by when these reports must be submitted. One must obtain these report formats in advance and seek clarification on parts which are difficult to understand, in order to avoid delays which may arise if clarifications are sought just at the expiry of the deadline. Also, it is wise to know the timeline expectation of the donor for project completion or phase completion.

> ➤ With this knowledge on timelines and quantifiables, one must then put in place methods to measure the end-results and track goal

achievement against the donor's timelines. Additionally, a process/method must be set in place to extract data and present it in the donor's format/s.

➢ MOUs (Memorandum of Understanding) with a donor is an absolute must-do, especially for mid-size to large donors. These MOUs must specify what the obligations/achievables are for both the donor and donee (or grantor and grantee), as well as the measurables or impact assessments and how they are to be carried out. If a project is a time-bound project, then the MOU must lock in the donor's commitment till project completion or else till a specified date. The MOU can also provide for the timelines for donations (whether upfront or in a phased manner). The MOU basically helps to nail down the majority of the uncertainties in the relationship and not leave them to later interpretation. An MOU helps to reduce the donor 'flight risk'.

It is absolutely imperative that we understand that the donors end-result and donors image management are not their sole responsibility or burden. These become one of our end-results/goals too, because if we fail in our endeavour the donor's failure is a given too, in what is nothing short of a domino effect. If your donor is an individual, then he or she could be a mighty sore loser if you fail. If your donor is an agency, those who have donated to the agency for your project will ask some mighty uncomfortable questions to the agency management. Net effect in either scenario – kiss your donors (and all future projects, too) goodbye!!

Manage your donor risk – it's not an option, it's an essential!

Chapter VI

Taxation Risk

The world over today, NGOs, corporates and even individuals are subjected - on an ever-increasing basis – to the microscope of taxation and its ever-widening tentacles. Gone are the days when you paid 'X' sum of tax on 'Y' sum of income/profit and 'you're home and dry'.

Taxation today has become akin to that monstrous python coiling itself in ever tightening rings around the business person, the corporate, the salaried and even the charitable NGO. The taxman's philosophy for the NGO seems to have become 'by all means do good, but pay tax'!!

Taxation began with the plain and simple income tax, followed by the Sales Tax (central or state) and then Value Added Tax (VAT), excise duties, octroi, customs, ADD (anti-dumping duties) and the latest bugbear in India – the GST (Goods & Service Tax). Taxation has permeated every aspect of human life. I do not doubt that soon there will be a tax imposed merely for living – we are already taxed when we are born (our parents paid tax on hospital bills). Fortunately, GST is exempted on funeral services, else we would be taxed even when we die.

Yet, come what may, the aspect of taxation is here to stay – it cannot be wished away and is one of the most serious risks any NGO faces. Receiving a notice from Income Tax ranks quite high up there in the list of nightmares for any NGO manager/finance head. You simply never know what to expect when you slit the official looking brown envelope or when you flip open the folded IT notice. Rarely does a smile cross one's face. More often than not the expression is either one of dismay or else utter confusion.

There are so many sections under which IT notices can be issued and what makes these sections more horrifying to handle is the legalese with which each section is written. Indeed, only those with a flair for the English language, a legal bent of mind and a love for punctuation, will most likely find the reading of Income Tax law more interesting than a Perry Mason thriller.

IT notices happen to be just one part of Income Tax law and compliance that the average NGO faces today. The NGO's brush with Income Tax begins, of course, right at the very beginning – ab ipso initio. It begins with the necessity to register with the Income Tax department and obtain a Tax file number or Permanent Account Number (PAN). After obtaining a PAN, you need to quote it when opening a bank account, when depositing cash into bank – above a certain limit, etc. Then you must file Income Tax returns at the end of the financial year against that PAN Number/IT File and then wait for it to be assessed by IT authorities. If your IT returns are selected for detailed scrutiny, you can look forward to a good number of queries in the process of the scrutiny, information submissions and further queries.

That's just the Income Tax registration and returns part. Then comes the Tax Deduction at Source (TDS) part, wherein, if you are issuing contracts, work orders or have employees who are assessable to tax on salaries, you need to comply with Income Tax law relating to deducting tax at source, on sums paid to different categories of persons and then remitting this TDS to the government. This activity is followed by the need to comply with the rules for filing returns on TDS deducted & TDS paid to the govt – on quarterly and annual basis.

With just these 6 introductory paragraphs on taxation, I sincerely believe that I would have been successful in inducing at least a mild headache in you. There is no escaping the long arm of taxation and there is certainly no avoiding the headaches that go with it. Taxation presents a very serious risk for the NGO, compounded by the fact that many NGOs lack skilled resource persons to deal with this massive area of compliance.

What are the risks of non-compliance or half-baked compliance with Income Tax laws? For one, you could lose your PAN number – it could be suspended or cancelled altogether. Once that happens, your PAN status in your NGO's bank account will in due course show up as 'unregistered' or suspended and tax becomes applicable at the rate of 20% on your incomes. You may even lose your bank account, in which case you can only deal in cash and consistently dealing in cash above the threshold limits could attract penal action from the Income Tax Dept., and the government – all the while exposing you to 'cash risk' (refer Financial Risk in Chapter III).

Half-baked compliance such as not deducting TDS or deducting it late (in a subsequent quarter or two quarters later) or filing late IT returns will invite strong penalties from Income Tax by way of 'Interest on late payment' as well as penalty, not to forget the infringement going on record in your tax file. The interest amount could be high – substantially high.

Improper responses to queries during IT returns assessment could lead to penalties being levied ranging from token sums to astronomical amounts running into millions of rupees, and in a scenario where you need to pay first and appeal later, such penalties can break the back of the organisation.

So how does one go about dealing with this beast called Income Tax? Compliance with Income Tax starts at the beginning – ab ipso initio.

Commencement compliance: As soon as your NGO is registered in the eyes of law (becomes a legal entity – whether Trust, Society or Section 8 company), you need to register your legal entity with Income Tax – i.e. apply for a Tax file number or PAN number for your new legally recognised person/entity.

This is done by either: i) applying online or (ii) downloading the specified application form and submitting it at the authorised facilitation centres.

The relevant form is Form 49A.

<u>Online application process:</u> Online PAN application can be made at the website address – https://tin.tin.nsdl.com/pan/index.html or https://www.utiitsl.com/UTIITSL_SITE/pan/index.html

These two entities (NSDL and UTIITSL) have been authorised by Income Tax authorities to process PAN applications.

Follow the instructions, fill in your entity's data in the relevant fields, upload scanned copies of the relevant documents, sign the form with a digital signature certificate (DSC) (Class II or III DSC) and submit.

<u>Manual application process:</u> The manual application process applies for those entities and individuals who are not comfortable with the online process and/or do not have a Class II or III DSC (which most people do not). In such a case, you visit the Income Tax website.

Download the Form 49A, print the form, fill in the details while following the instructions provided from page 3 onwards. Attach the relevant documents and submit the filled in form at a nearby TIN facilitation centre of UTIITSL or NSDL and obtain an acknowledgement from them after payment of the applicable fee.

In either case (online/manual), you will need to provide the Aadhar card details and copies of the trustees/governing body members/etc. This is mandatory as per law (recent Supreme Court of India ruling on 26th September 2018).

You will need to await instructions via SMS/email for any errors in your PAN application or confirmation that PAN has been issued. If there are documentation errors, you will need to submit relevant documents asked for by the IT authorities or else re-submit the entire application form again. Once the PAN number is issued, the PAN Card will then be couriered to the registered address you had mentioned in the application form.

Registration under sections 12A & 12AA: Almost all NGOs are formed for carrying out some charitable purpose or the other. Some NGOs are religious bodies which also do charitable works as a direct extension or in practice of one or more of the tenets of their faith/ religious beliefs. Such NGOs are religious and charitable. The Income Tax Act defines charitable purposes in Section 2(15) of the Act. Each NGO necessarily receives income from various sources – incomes which are assessable to tax, including interest on fixed deposits. Any NGO worth its salt would not want it's incomes earned to be subjected to taxation and a considerable sum taken away by the taxman, particularly when the application of incomes towards charitable causes would be more noble and effective in the alleviation of social ills – which after all, is the purpose for which the NGO was established. Hence NGOs seek exemption from taxation from the IT authorities by registering under section 12A of the Income Tax Act, which is a one-time registration. However, such exemption can only be sought if you are first registered with the Income Tax authorities under Section 12 & 12 AA of the Income Tax act. For a new NGO, this should be done preferably at the time of PAN application with the IT authorities. For an existing one without such 12A registration, application should be made immediately without delay. An application for registration under 12A should include 12AA as well, which though procedural in nature, provides the NGO with an exemption from GST (see GST services booklet Serial No. 1 in the List of Services at NIL Rate) for most NGOs. Sec 12AA came into effect from 1st April 1997.

Routine Operational Taxation compliance: If one ran the NGO with corporate jargon acronyms, this one would be referred to as ROTC. In simple terms, routine operational tax compliance covers deduction of tax from vendors/contractors/employee payments and remitting this to the government within the applicable deadlines and as per the laid down rules for deduction. Along with this, one must submit the required quarterly and annual returns or reports to the government. Here's how you go about it.

First, you need to apply for a TAN number or a Tax Deduction and Collection Account Number. This is a ten-digit alpha-numeric number under which TDS deductions must be made and paid to the government. The quarterly returns must also be filed under this number.

- Categories of deductions at source: There are various categories of assessees or persons, to whom we make payments from which we must deduct TDS before making payment. These most common categories are contractors (u/s 194C), consultants (u/s 194J), employees (u/s 192B), rent (u/s 194I), and so on. The other categories are found in the 'Notes' page or page 2 of the ITNS 281 Challan for TDS payment. These categories are then broadly classified based on their constitution – (a) individual/ proprietorship (non-company); (b) partnership (non-company); (c) Limited/Private Limited (company).

- Rates of TDS: The rates for tax deduction at source are as follows. On contractors & vendors who are proprietorship firms or individuals TDS is deductible @1%. On contractors & vendors who are partnership firms or private limited or public limited concerns TDS is deductible @2%. For professionals or technical service persons or consultants, the rate is 10%.

- TDS on employee salaries: For employees a separate calculation structure needs to be put in place which factors in the employee's salary, exemption limit, standard deductions, investments and permissible deductions under various sections and the slabs of taxation and their applicable rates. This is an ongoing role and needs checking from month-to-month, with particularly detailed scrutiny being necessary in the last 4 months of the financial year. Another aspect of TDS on employee salaries is that deductions must not be back-ended or loaded on/recovered in the last 3 months of the year. For example, if employee X is assessed as taxable for a total tax of Rs. 15000 in a financial year, as employers we must not recover the TDS in the last 3 months of the financial year as Rs. 5000 × 3. Law dictates that ideally this should be spaced out proportionately/uniformly over year (i.e. Rs. 1250 p.m. × 12 months). This is meant to ease the burden on the employee and spread the tax liability uniformly. In case of any extra amount deductible as TDS or non-submission of tax-deductible investments proof by the employer, then the employee's TDS shortfall can be deducted at the end of the financial year.

- <u>Remitting to government</u>: The TDS deducted from the various categories of deductees needs to be remitted to the government on monthly basis, though not in the same month as the month in which deduction is made. For example, TDS deducted in June needs to be paid to the government by 7th of the next month following the month of deduction – i.e. July. These payments to the Income Tax authorities/government are made through Challan ITNS 281 – which may or may not be accompanied by a cheque (depending upon your banker's rules & regulations). However, the aspect of remitting TDS to the government is one area of operational compliance risk where most of us might slip up. Many may assume that they have 7 days in which to pay the money to the government, though in my opinion the seventh day should not be counted. Invariably in those seven days, one day will be a Sunday. *Submitting your ITNS challan to your bank on the 7th day of the month is the equivalent to submitting yourself to a very big risk. Some banks are prone to 'link failures', or some clerk/officer putting your instruction into a drawer or file at the time of submission and forgetting about it or some other unforeseen error.* The fact of the matter is that IT authorities' systems have in the past few years been upgraded and enhanced by Information Technology. TDS remitted to the government on the 8th day of the following month, is a late submission according to the IT authorities' info-tech systems. A clearing cheque submitted for TDS remittance, on day 6 gets cleared on day 8 and received by the govt on day 9 – again a late payment. Needless to say, late payments to the government are liable for penalties & penal interest on late payment. These are some of the classic operational taxation compliance risks we unwittingly subject our organisations to.

- Form 16: For an employee from whom TDS has been deducted during the financial year, this is a certificate which must be issued to him/her stating the amount of salary paid, tax deductible savings made by the employee, TDS deducted and remitted to government. The form 16 comes in 2 parts – Part A & Part B. Form 16 is an annual certificate issued once a year – on or before 15th June – after the end of the financial year. Without the Form 16 your employee will find it very difficult to file his or her Annual Income Tax return, in the absence of the required details. One important aspect to be noted, is that if no TDS is deducted from your employee during the financial year you are not liable or bound to issue a Form 16 – a simple certificate of annual salary (on company letterhead) is sufficient.

- Form 16A: In a similar manner to the Form 16, the Form 16A is issued to non-employees such as contractors, consultants, vendors, lessors, etc. Essentially it is a certificate for TDS on incomes other than salary. Form 16A is a certificate that must be issued on a quarterly basis.

- Quarterly returns submission 24Q: For employees, TDS is deducted uniformly (more or less) throughout the financial year and is remitted to the government accordingly. A report for the same needs to be submitted to the government every quarter through a Form 24Q. This Form 24Q has 2 parts to it – Annexure I and Annexure II. Annexure I has to be submitted for all 4 quarters of the financial year while Annexure II is to be submitted only in the last quarter.

- Quarterly returns submission 26Q: For TDS deducted on non-salary payments, a separate set of quarterly returns to be submitted to the government which is known as the 26Q.

With routine taxation compliance for vendors & employees, one must be especially careful to submit returns (24Q & 26Q) on time and correctly. The compliance risk here lies not in the scrutiny by any individual (read assessing officer). When submitting these returns, you are pitted directly against a computer system/software (called TRACES), which is capable of catching the smallest errors such as late payments, errors in returns and levying penalties and interest on late payments, too. Most of the IT notices get shot off by the software.

That is, of course, not to say that this software is perfect – it does have its flaws, as after all any software depends on the rules on which it is built as these define its limitations. Any and all software has boundaries/limitations – after all, it is no human being.

Annual Taxation compliance: Once you have registered for a PAN number, as an NGO, you are assessable to tax – whether you like it or not. Every year by 30th September, you need to file the Annual IT Return for your organisation. The Annual IT return is a summation of the incomes and expenditure of your organisation; stated in the format laid down by the tax authorities; and your resulting tax liability, if any. At the time of computing your tax liability, one needs to factor in the exemption from taxation for which you have registered with the IT authorities under Section 12A & 12AA. Also, the provisions listed in your annual exemption certificate obtained from Income Tax (on various sources of income) during the year will come into play while calculating your taxation liability/refund of tax deducted.

The risk in Annual Taxation compliance lies in the IT returns not being computed as per the provisions of income tax law or in the annual returns not being submitted on time. Annual returns prepared and submitted at 00:01 on 1st October of any year, will invite a late filing penalty from Income Tax (unless the last date for filing is extended beyond 30th Sept). This one-minute delay may have occurred due to link failure, server downtime, your error, etc but it will cost you. A couple of paragraphs earlier, I had mentioned how the IT returns process was system/software driven. Since a software runs on bits and bytes, 0s and 1s, it will not recognise a momentary link failure or some other seemingly valid reason. A return submitted at 11:59:59 pm on 30th Sept is within the filing deadline, while that of 00:00:01 on 1st October, is after the deadline and technically a late return.

Annual Exemption certificate: Most NGOs apply every year to the IT authorities for an Exemption Certificate, which allows for zero tax deduction on their interest incomes, rental incomes, etc. Merely having a 12A registration is not sufficient, an additional application in the prescribed format (with relevant supporting documents) is necessary too. The IT authorities, on being satisfied with the credentials of the applicant, may issue the exemption certificate. Copies of the exemption certificate are then sent (by the IT authorities) to the relevant organisations/companies/individuals, with whom your NGO has dealings, telling them to deduct no TDS (or deduct TDS at a concessional rate) on sums paid to your NGO. It is imperative that your NGO apply for and obtain the exemption certificate, else a substantial portion of your incomes could be subjected to tax at source, resulting in the risk of lower incomes and the risk of higher project deficits. TDS deducted at source can be claimed as refundable in the Annual return but the refund is likely to happen 12–18 months later.

Professional Tax compliance: Another aspect of taxation compliance is Professional Tax. When you employ people in your NGO, you become liable for the deduction of Profession Tax (or PTax) by way of it being an 'employment'. Every month you will be required to deduct Professional Tax, from the employee, at the time of disbursement of salary and remit the tax to the State government within the specified deadline. Each state in India has a separate P.Tax Act under which the rates for deduction of Professional Tax is specified. Different salary slabs attract different rates of Profession Tax. The compliance risk here lies in not deducting the Professional Tax from employees' payments, at the time of payment and/or P Tax which has been deducted not being remitted to the state government or not remitted on time. In addition to the deduction of P.Tax and remittance to the authorities, the NGO also needs to submit an annual P.Tax return to the government.

TDS on real estate purchase: One lesser known taxation compliance that applies to most NGOs is that of TDS on real estate purchases – applicable since June 2013 – where the value of the purchase is greater than Rs. 50 lakhs. Most NGOs purchase property (land or land and building) at some time or the other for conduct of their social sector activities. At the time of purchase of such property and making payment to the seller, the buyer (i.e. the NGO in this case) is required by law to make a certain minimum deduction for TDS (1%) on the consideration/sale value and deposit this with the government. Failure to do so can attract penalties since property purchase is generally a high value transaction.

Employee Perquisites: Many organisations offer their employees various perquisites as sweeteners to engage their services (get them to join the organisation) or work longer hours. In some cases, perquisites become a method to increase an employee's remuneration (read as CTC or 'Cost to Company'), without increasing their tax liability. Many of these perquisites can be taxable as per tax law and in many cases, there will be instances of the record of perquisites not being maintained and if maintained, not included in the employee's taxation calculations. More than corporates, our NGOs need to exercise greater caution when it comes to employee perquisites and their taxation aspects.

- - - - -

These are just some of the basic aspects of tax compliance and with non-compliance you run the risk of a number of penalties prescribed in the Income Tax Act. I am sure that none of us, as leaders and managers of NGOs, wish to be identified as offenders/repeat offenders in the eyes of income tax authorities – as frequent fliers in the halls of tax delinquency. It's bad for business and bad for our image.

Taxation compliance isn't rocket science, it's more a lot of legal understanding and meticulousness.

Knowing what to do is more than half the battle won.
Getting it done is the remaining part of the battle.

Chapter VII

FCRA Risks

This sectoral risk is one of the biggies for the NGO/third sector in India. In the last couple of years, thousands of NGOs have lost their FCRA registrations – either suspended or cancelled. A couple of foreign donor agencies (one very well-known one too) have also been blocked from sending grants and donations to India.

However, that's not to say that the foreign donations have fallen to zero on account of the registration cancellations or suspensions. Across the world, there are individuals and charitable organisations/agencies whose core values are centred on the principles of philanthropy and helping those in need or addressing critical global needs. It mostly stems from Abraham Maslow's final step/stage in the Hierarchy of Needs – which tells us that when people reach that certain stage in life where once their basic, physiological, social and self-esteem needs are met, they need to give back to society in a bid for self-actualisation.

That is the primary rationale behind philanthropy. As long as there are wealthy foreigners (even NRIs) there will be donations made across the globe for 'worthy causes' and India happens to be one of the focus nations for those wealthy causes.

How is it that donations (or grants) from foreigners or foreign entities are a source of potential risk? After all, foreign donors are the greatest source of funds for NGOs in India. Every organisation with an FCRA registration knows that.

The source of the risk lies in the regulations/laws. Non-profits receiving funds from foreign donors are subject to regulation by the government through the provisions of the Foreign Contribution Regulation Act (FCRA) 2010 (and earlier to the FCRA Act 1976).

While most NGOs cannot wait to rush into the foreign funding territory (i.e. FCRA realm) this area of non-profit activity is thick with regulations & reporting requirements – as mentioned earlier in Chapter II – a veritable labyrinth placed in a minefield.

The resultant effect of receiving foreign funds and not complying with the regulations laid down in the FCRA Act, is suspension/cancellation of FCRA licence and even, possible imprisonment and fines.

Laid down below are some of the simple (yet costly) mistakes that an NGO can make in relation to foreign funds and the FCRA Act.

Receiving foreign funds without FCRA permission: No NGO is authorised to receive foreign funds without first obtaining the permission of the Central Government (more specifically the Ministry of Home Affairs – FCRA division) (MoHA). If the foreign funds to be received are a regular affair, then one needs to apply to the MoHA for a FCRA registration number. The relevant application form needs to be submitted along-with details of the governing body members/trustees and audited annual accounts, as well as the entity's registration certificate, Memorandum/Articles or Trust Deed, Audited Accounts for last 3 years, Section 12A registration certificate, etc.

Before applying for registration, you need to open a FCRA bank account (preferably with a Scheduled Bank) and mention the account number in your FCRA application form. Once registration is obtained, your banker will be sent a notice by the MoHA informing them of the grant of FCRA registration and only after that will the bank allow the account to be operated and foreign funds to be credited therein.

If the foreign funds are a one-off case and not to be a regular one, you need to apply for a 'prior permission' from MoHA. The prior permission allows you to receive the funds from a particular donor once or in multiple tranches over a specified period of time. Once these funds are received (upto the specified amount), the bank will stop crediting any foreign funds to your FCRA bank account, as any excess credit would amount a violation of the FCRA laws by the bank.

Multiple accounts for FCRA funds: An NGO which is granted a FCRA registration can receive foreign funds only into ONE FCRA designated bank account. One entity cannot have two or more FCRA accounts – this is a gross violation of FCRA law. Only one FCRA account is permitted so that the MoHA has a reporting control on how much each FCRA registered entity is receiving over a period of time. (Banks are required to submit regular information returns to the MoHA). Multiple accounts are only permitted in the case of 'project/branch accounts' *for disbursement or utilization* of funds for specific projects based at locations far from the head-office. Even these multiple disbursement/utilization accounts have strict rules for operation/compliance.

Non-maintenance of separate set of books of accounts for FC funds: A common mistake easily made by newcomers to the FCRA Act and process is to maintain a single set of books of accounts for both FCRA funds and non-FCRA funds. This is not permitted by the FCRA Act and a separate set of books of accounts must be kept for FCRA funds (receipts & payments). This set of books of accounts (FC) must be audited every year and the audited accounts must form a part of the FC Utilization statement sent to the MoHA every year within the specified deadline. Non-compliance with this requirement will lead to the compliance risk mentioned next.

Mixing FC funds with local: For any NGO with an FCRA registration, all funds received can be categorised into 'foreign funds' and 'local rupee funds'. As the saying goes "East is East and West is

West, and ne'er the twain shall meet", so shall foreign funds and local rupee funds NEVER be mixed. Mixing such funds would mean local rupee funds being deposited into an FCRA Bank Account – which is generally quite difficult as banks are quite vigilant on FCRA accounts these days. The reverse is not difficult – the deposit of foreign funds into a local rupee account. How is this even a possibility? some might ask. When an NGO's management incorrectly classify a receipt from a foreign source as a non-foreign donation, then it gets deposited into the local rupee bank account. Alternately, incorrect bank details provided to a foreign donor and the banker for the local rupee bank account does not query the source of funds being credited, may result in foreign funds credited to a local rupee bank account.

Also maintaining a single set of books of accounts for both foreign & local rupee funds, is likely to exacerbate the possibility of this single greatest FC error.

FC Returns not filed (quarterly/annually): As an NGO, once an FCRA registration is received from the MoHA, you become duty bound to submit reports/returns to the MoHA at various intervals. The first set of reports is the Quarterly FC return wherein you must provide details of the foreign funds received during the last quarter and mention the donor details (name, address & email ID) as well as the purpose of the donation (i.e. Social/Religious/Educational, etc). This report must be filed online by the 15th of each month following the quarter end (i.e. filed by 15th July for the April – May – June quarter, and so on).

In the event that you have not received any foreign funds during the quarter, you must still file the return – though as a NIL return.

If no foreign funds are received for 2 successive years you are liable to lose your registration. Therefore, one must always be cautious of this aspect and ensure that at least one FC donation happens in a year – even if it be a meagre $ 50.

It is important to mention here that interest received on Fixed Deposits (placed from foreign funds) from a Bank (and credited to the FC account) also form part of FC receipts during that quarter. If such interest is received and not reported, it could be construed by the MoHA as a reporting violation or worse, as a concealment of foreign funds.

There is also an annual FC return to be submitted each year, after the foreign set of books of accounts are audited. This return is to be submitted online by 31st December each year, along with an audited set of FC accounts and other documents. Failure to submit annual returns can (and will) lead to cancellation of FCRA registration. This is one of the primary reasons quoted for cancellation of many NGO FC registrations.

Foreign funds used for disallowed/risky purposes: The FCRA act expressly forbids the use of foreign funds for the hospitality of foreign nationals. Yet there will be NGOs receiving foreign funds and making the mistake of booking the expenses of visiting overseas guests/donors from foreign funds.

Another disallowed or 'frowned upon' use for foreign funds is investment in property deals which are short to medium term in nature. These can be classified as 'speculative' investments. In my view, investment in property (read land and buildings or only land) is an investment ideally for a long-term purpose. NGOs are not deep pocket entities or corporates which can deploy seriously big money for investment in property without that property having a 'solid fit' with the organization's objectives/goals. A question that must be posed here is would we invest 5 million rupees on a piece of land for 3 years if that 5 million could be spent on achieving the organization's goals in 2 years?? That's a no-brainer really. Once a property to be purchased has a 'solid fit' with the organisation's objectives, there is logically no way it should be sold before 8–10 years are over (or more) unless the organization goes belly-up or the project for which it was purchased has hit a 'Mt. Everest'. Yet there are NGOs that put money into property which is sold in the medium term – 'investments' which are clearly speculative in nature. In doing so, you are doing the equivalent of placing your FCRA licence on the roulette table.

Another avenue of risk that a few NGOs 'mistakenly' get into is utilizing FC funds for politically sensitive projects. A project such as 'clean water' is not a proverbial political hot potato, whereas the use of FC funds for food & refreshments for a community involved in protests against some politically sensitive issue is a no-go. In today's scenario of stringent regulatory scrutiny, it is always better to avoid the "path where angels fear to tread" than risk one's hard earned FC licence.

FC funds used for non-designated purpose/s: When an overseas donor sends funds to us, in 95% of the cases the donor will specify the purpose for which the funds are to be used. Process (and the unwritten rule) demands that these funds be used for the purpose/s which the donor specifies. It is wrong to assume that these funds can be utilized as per the whims and fancies (read decisions) of the governing body/trustees/directors. Many NGOs will make this mistake – of using designated funds for a non-designated purpose. A fund designated for "x" purpose can only be utilized for "y" purpose with the express permission of the donor. Changing the designation specification does not rest with the donee (i.e. you) but with the donor.

- - - - -

FCRA is one area of the NGO work-day wherein we need to constantly be on our toes. A seemingly innocent mistake on any day can lead to stoppage of funds for a decade (or more).

Chapter VIII

Human Capital Risk or Human Resources Risk

Each and every organisation – whether NGO or corporate (big or small) – operates on one very basic (and important) foundation/resource – the human resource. Provided below is some background information (drawn from another work/book of mine) on this resource – also known as "human capital".

The aspect of the human resource was first defined by management thinkers/gurus, merely to recognize the presence of the human element in the production process. This was the day and age of the post-industrial revolution, when resources were treated as key aspects in production. There were so many other resources/inputs in the production/economic process, which needed to be recognized. These are sometimes summed up as the M's of management – men, money, machines, materials, management, marketing, etc. Once the need arose to define the various elements/inputs in the production process, the need also arose to effectively control these various inputs, since each input/element was a contributor to the cost of production and the cost of production impacted the enterprise's profit. Since it all stemmed from the necessity to boost profit and increase economic value, economists and management gurus began to work down the chain of production to the various inputs in the process.

It all began as an effort to control the input costs of the various resources, including the human resource. Once the process of cost control over the human resource was achieved, the focus of managements then changed to improving the productivity and efficiency of all resources including the human resource.

Better remuneration, leisure time, subsidized meals, day care centers and so on followed – all to boost the productivity time and the efficiency of the man/woman behind the machine.

Next the world's economies made the paradigm shift from being product oriented to being service oriented. With the intangible called services taking root in the economies of the world, the brain began to become of greater importance and it began to play a greater role in the ever-growing GDP of each nation. Thus far, it was about the physical strength of the human resource but that was undergoing a marked transformation. No longer was the (physical) labourer in the field or in the factory considered the builder of society. It was now the knowledge worker – the white-collar worker – who assumed a greater importance in the new age economy of the world. The epicenter of economies began to shift from the farmyard to the 'firm-yard' and from rural to urban. It was the researcher, the scientist, the banker, the marketer, the teacher, the consultant, the manager, the CEO – net-net, the knowledge worker – who now held sway over the economies of the world.

Then began the era of training and development and mentoring and with it came delegation and empowering and grooming employees for future leadership roles. Training, development and mentoring are some of the corporate mantras that most CEOs will swear by, in today's day and age. There is hardly a corporate (worth its salt) which would like to admit that it doesn't train its staff and mentor future leaders. Every CEO or HR head would have some special agenda for the human resource in his or her organization – whether in letter or in spirit.

Treatment or handling or managing of the human resource has come a long, long way in the last couple of hundred years. Ranging from slave labour to the non-slave labourer, to the blue-collar worker to the 'employee' to personnel to human resources – staff have been classified differently with each passing wave of 'people management'.

The latest concept to take the world by storm is the regarding of the human resource as 'human capital'. With the advent of the services sector and it's forming a majority part of most economies, the human input factor in every economy/organization can hardly be denied. While we have moved on from the industrial era/economy to the knowledge economy (including the digital economy), the key input component is now knowledge which is primarily the output of the human brain.

Every one probably has some idea (however vague) as to what 'capital' is. One dictionary defines it quite well – 'stock with which company or person enters into business; accumulated wealth, esp. as used in further production'. *What, therefore, is 'human capital'?*

When a company enters business or is in business and is in continuous production, certain stock or financial wealth or value is required in order to commence production/functioning or to continue production or continue functioning. This stock, also referred to as economic value, may come to be in the possession of the company in so many varied ways. Some of the stock or economic value, which keeps the entity going may be money, investment in fixed assets such as factory, buildings, machinery, etc. Some of the economic value may come from holding stocks of various materials utilized in the production process such as raw materials, work-in-progress and even finished goods. All of these are a financial measure and economic value of the resources required to keep the company in production. There is however one very, very crucial resource whose value is yet to be effectively measured and quoted in the Balance Sheet of any company or organization – which is the Human resource. It is the easiest task of all to make a head-count of all the employees in the organization and state the same in the Balance Sheet, as a few companies do nowadays. It is however a Herculean task to assess and quantify the economic value of this resource – *which is by far the most important resource.* Despite its importance and criticality to the balance sheet, the human resource lies unmeasured. Yet it contributes more to any business topline or bottomline, than all the other resources put together. That contribution, my friends, is human capital – the quantified, measured economic value of the human resource.

Your human capital is the sum of the intellect, skills, knowledge, logic, common sense, commitment and ability which each of your people bring to your company/organization. The skills and abilities, the brain-power, the ingenuity, the integrity – all of these are components of human capital. It is not the financial power or mineral resource which an entity controls or commands which is the greatest capital, it is the human capital which is the greatest investment in any organization. Any company can have billions of dollars' worth of money for its capital. Minus the brains and the intellect to apply that billion dollars, all the money of the world, would remain just that – money – not capital, not a productive resource. All the resources of the world in fact are of zero value, without the human skill and ability to enable it to be converted into value.

The interpretation of law, management science, forming and shaping of interpersonal relationships, design and building and operation of machines, etc is all an output of the human brain or in other words the result of 'human capital'.

Human capital is what human capital does.

It takes the unproductive and idle resources and converts them into value – it is the conversion agent – the catalyst, without which any reaction (economic or social) would never be complete.

The difference, between the farmer of one economy who uses a plough and the farmer of another economy who uses a tractor, is not the money, which tells them apart or the GDP of their respective nations. The difference is not in the financial wealth of nations, nor in the competitive advantage of them, nor is the difference in the abundance of raw materials or anything else. The difference lies in the specialist behind the scenes, who designed the tractor, the finance head of the tractor company who made it available at an affordable price and the machine-shop floor worker who helped manufacture the machine. The difference between any two nations lies in the level of knowledge and application of that knowledge towards the betterment of that nation. Knowledge in itself yields no reward, except when applied. *That knowledge and its application, through human skill, is human capital.*

A nation rich in wealth has only become rich by the application of its knowledge. If its human capital is high and well developed, the nation is rich. A nation, which is poor, is so because the level of knowledge is low, in turn stunting the level of application of knowledge. A poor or under-developed nation will remain thus until the level of knowledge improves and with it the level of application of knowledge.

The quality, success ranking and sustainability of any organisation depends first and foremost on the quality, quantity of its human capital component and how it manages that human capital resource within itself.

When giving cognizance to the realm of human resources/human capital, the NGO is no different from the corporate. In an NGO, success and failure depend on the human capital it employs and how well it manages that human capital and the value it obtains from that human capital. Every project the NGO undertakes requires staff to reach it to its end-beneficiaries and administer the project and ensure functioning of the overall organisation. Its human capital is the resource which defines its objectives, translates the objectives into plans, implements those plans, administers itself and carries the plans to completion among the target set of beneficiaries and finally providing for measurement of the success ratios of the entire activity. *In the NGO, the delivery vehicle for the entire social agenda is the human capital component.*

Therefore, it follows that the quantum, quality & management of this human capital will make a world of difference from one NGO to another and therein lies the human capital risk for the social sector.

Most NGOs give very little cognizance to this precious resource. To them most of the staff are just employees who represent a necessary monthly financial burden. Most NGO leaders & managers are still operating in the post-industrial revolution stage having just begun to consider the value of their human resources. There are some NGOs, though, which place high value on their people – enabling them, empowering them and making full use of their skill sets & intellectual capital. These few are the newer NGOs not steeped in tradition.

Enumerated below are some of the factors which impact our human capital thereby enhancing the human capital risk in our NGOs.

Quantum of human capital – Some NGOs employ a lot of people to get their work done. The mere presence of people in your workforce does not automatically translate into human capital. In other words, more people are NOT equal to more human capital. In fact, I have found the reverse to be true. Having a lot of or too many staff often translates into less human capital as per capita productivity is lower, managerial attention is divided over too many, monitoring is less and scope of all-round training and development of human capital is greatly diminished. With a greater breadth of human resources, the depth of human capital in such a scenario tends to be shallow. Moreover, it leads to another risk which is of a financial nature. Too many staff mean greater deployment of money towards to a less productive resource. In other words, a good resource (money) wasted on a less productive one which translates into a double whammy for the NGO – lower productivity coupled with higher cost.

On the flip side, having too few staff in an organization may defeat the purpose of the NGO's objective. Too few people in the organisation results in greater stress/load on 'less-than-optimal' human capital, resulting in greater stretching of human resources giving rise to fatigue, demoralisation and the resultant inability to deliver the desired effects on the goals/objectives of the NGO. (Remember what was said a couple of paragraphs earlier about human capital as the 'delivery vehicle'). In a bottomline strategy similar to the corporates – there is a resulting trade-off between financial risk and goal achievement risk. In the NGO we must strive to find that optimal level or trade-off between numbers and cost.

Quality of human capital – Not only is quantity an important factor, the **quality** of staff is equally integral to the organisation's human capital risk. Having too many unqualified staff or incompetent staff serves to undermine the foundations of the organisation from the very get-go, as the knowledge factor/ratio starts in the negative zone. Taking a negative 'human-capital-to-knowledge-ratio' and converting this into a zero value is by any means a steep uphill task and moving the barometer, thereafter, from zero into greater positive territory is another monumental achievement altogether. Every NGO needs to have a bare minimum number of qualified staff in its upper echelons and middle management. No organisation can boast of having 100% skilled/qualified staff in these two tiers – not even the corporates. However, in my opinion, a minimum of 60% skilled/qualified staff need to fill these two critical tiers of management in the NGO. Quality levels of human capital are crucial since when it comes to extraction of the best from human capital, the organisation can only extract that (i.e. knowledge) which is there for extraction. *Extraction from nothing results in nothing.* Mining of low-grade mineral ore can only yield low grade mineral.

The lack of quality of human capital can seriously set an NGO back in terms of goal achievement – in fact this aspect of human capital will make the difference between an NGO's success and its woe-begotten attempts to achieve anything.

Every NGO worth its salt must establish its own 'Talent Acquisition Plan' wherein it recognises the skill sets required of its human resources in each unit/department in the middle management and top management tiers. It must then set about actively acquiring such talent through proper purpose-driven recruitment.

At the time of recruiting human resources, NGO managers & leaders must take special care to avoid employing their own 'special/ favoured' candidates or 'stocking the larder with yes men'. Or for that matter selection of candidates as employees based on 'compassion'. 'Compassionate recruitment' can kill an NGO's future by killing its human capital base – simply because compassion recruits are recruits who were unemployable elsewhere, which is why they were not picked up by someone else. *If you are picking from leftovers, you can expect nothing but someone else's rejects.*

The recruitment must be driven totally by the provisions/requirements of the Talent Acquisition Plan, else there is no point in venturing down this road at all. The NGO might as well stay where it is and collect moss and decay over time.

Inadequate remuneration – Many NGOs cannot afford to pay (or choose not to pay) market related salaries or even 'half-market-related' salaries. This is one deadly factor that contributes big-time to the human capital risk for the NGO and makes for the classic chicken and egg story. Poor remuneration levels will result in the inability to attract quality human capital – which obviously finds the corporate pay package (and the sectoral challenges) more attractive. It's a no-brainer, really.

The inability to recruit quality human capital because of poor remuneration packages results in low skill levels, archaic methods being employed, inefficiency, low human-capital-knowledge-ratio and the NGO generally operating in the 'age-of-the-dinosaur'.

Another negative side to the low remuneration factor is that there's a high degree of grumbling among employees (better classified as 'bitching') about the organisation. Demoralisation follows the grumbling and soon a general lethargy about everything takes root among the staff, followed by an aversion to doing anything positive. Such a scenario reminds me of a 'prisoner of war camp' from the film Bridge on the River Kwai – only in this case it's a disguised forceful incarceration, paid for in pennies.

Paying decent remuneration can attract corporate talent – people who are looking to do something by way of 'giving back to society'. Even young talent looking to go 'off the beaten path' will find the NGO/social sector attractive and can boost the organisation's success/ by bring in cutting edge ideas.

Lack of training/skill development – The absence of a strong training/skill development programme in the NGO/social sector organisation can effectively render almost every staff member 'obsolete' in 10–15 years. Imagine not sharpening an axe for months on end but attempting to cut wood with it on a daily basis. The world keeps moving on in terms of practices, procedures and technology. The digital technology of last week becomes redundant next week.

To stand still in the midst of the world's continuous forward motion is the equivalent of going in reverse when others are going forward.

Nothing frustrates human capital greater than the brainless choice to live in a Jurassic World during the age of Artificial Intelligence. In order to keep our human capital at par (or even closely updated) with progress we NGO managers and leaders need to ensure relevant & frequent training for our human capital. That very vital resource – human capital – cannot be subjected to the risk of redundancy in a dynamic world. After all, human capital is what human capital does. If our human capital is rendered redundant or obsolete in the face of the world's technology, we therefore have rendered ourselves (our NGOs) redundant in an increasingly modern scenario.

Training and skill development are all the more critical in today's NGO world, given that donors requirements and demands are ever increasing and more technology based. A donor functioning in digital mode will not take kindly to our functioning in 'paper-mode'.

Additionally, regulatory compliance is becoming more and more complex and stringent with each passing week. With the introduction of the global FATF (Financial Action Task Force) post 9/11, rules and regulations are constantly changing in the realms of banking, finance, legal compliance, FCRA, Taxation, etc. As a fallout of 9/11, KYC & FATCA are important features of banking process today not to forget the cross-border exchange of information on 'black money' stashed in numbered 'Swiss' accounts.

In India, for Foreign Currency receipts, FCRA registered entities are required to periodically confirm to the bankers on whether any of the FC receipts are from specifically banned/watchlist countries.

All of this is not to forget the ever-present global phenomenon of 'action in one part of the world, reaction in another part of the world'. One such example of this phenomenon is the escalating trade-war rhetoric and actions between USA and China, having definitive (and serious) negative impacts on South East Asian countries and India.

All of this economic dynamism calls for our top and middle management human capital to be (and stay) upgraded and updated on global developments and how to deal with their impact on the NGO, through training and skill development.

Politics and the human capital – We must strive to ensure that our workplaces in NGOs are by and large free of politics. Human capital CANNOT flourish in a politically charged environment.

The playing of politics will always exist in our (and every) organisations – whether corporate, government or NGO. However, on a scalar representation of 1 to 10, the level or depth of politics should never exceed a 3 or a 3.5 (with 10 representing a highly politics centric environment). The reason I raise the political snake is that high levels of politics defeat the goals of the NGO by proving to be demotivating to real professionals (i.e. quality human capital). It hinders the achievement of the 'Super-ordinate goal' or the organisation's primary goal.

True professionals do not care for this time-wasting with organisational & inter-personal politics – what drives them is the achievement of the goal set for the organisation. While remuneration is important, the real professional draws greater satisfaction from goal-achievement than remuneration. At the end of the day, the satisfaction from a job well done proves to be a stronger adrenaline rush than a monetary bonus.

Either the NGO wastes the professional/human capital it has engaged in the playing of politics or it utilises it more productively towards the organisation's objectives. There are many NGOs/social sector organisations which would rather indulge in politics (and the crab mentality) than freely allow its human capital to focus on the NGO's achievement of the 'Super-ordinate goal'.

Interestingly the scope of organisational politics includes the aspect of partiality and unfair bias.

Inconducive environments for human capital – Once an NGO has recruited good quality human capital at adequate/fair remuneration, it must at all cost ensure to provide an environment that is conducive for human capital to do what it does. Aside from a non-political environ, the NGO leadership/management must ensure to avoid applying the policy of "do what I tell you, don't do as I do". Hypocrisy is one sure fire way to kill morale of human capital. *Telling your one-downs or senior colleagues to do what they are told (not what the chairperson/ director does) essentially means it is an organisation with DOUBLE STANDARDS.* It indicates that top leadership will tell you what to do but will not follow the same scale as the human capital is being told to follow.

Neither should human capital at work in an NGO ever be told "just do what I tell you, you are not paid to think". The very rationale for the recruitment of quality human capital is the application of intellect/ knowledge in the furtherance of the organisation's goals. Derision is another sure-fire way to kill the morale of human capital and it serves merely to blunt its cutting edge.

The resultant effect will be that your human capital will become pre-occupied with skirting decisions that fall squarely in the 'high-caution' zone, becoming more and more bureaucratic every day. Bureaucracy happens to be the worst enemy of human capital.

There is another aspect to conducive environments for human capital that has taken centre-stage of late with the Me-Too movement coming to the fore. I call it 'Sex, lies & videotape'. Sexual liaison, flirtations, office romances and extra-marital affairs all happen in some form or other in many corporates. When people work in close proximity for extended durations with others of the opposite sex (even the same sex), likings and dis-likings are bound to occur. The dis-liking generally leads to office politics and back-stabbing. The likings can develop into something more serious such as senior leadership people abusing their power & position in the organisation for indulging in sexual harassment, sexual liaison (and extra-marital affairs) with colleagues/juniors.

The funny aspect to this is these 'things' happen in NGOs too. While NGOs are social sector entities/organisations, I believe that their primary objective is to achieve goals of social development & upliftment – generally for the underprivileged sections of society. We are called to 'social development' not to 'sordid socialising' in the social sector entities.

While these 'special relationships' play out on centre-stage in the NGO, they tend to have a debilitating effect on human capital and its performance. The human capital observes such happenings and in a very short time begin to question how these special relationships can be permitted to flourish and why the management of the NGO don't crack down on these things. They begin to question the leeway given to these people and why they are permitted to get away with these things during office hours. The accountability of the people in question and their abuse of power and the lack of will-power of the top management to stop such happenings are reviewed next.

The result – demotivation, demoralization and a general tendency to become laid-back and not bring their full skill sets to the table any more. The human capital begins to look for the next BBD (bigger better deal) and soon flies out the door.

- - - - -

Without realising it, NGOs face a very palpable risk in terms of human capital and it is absolutely high time and imperative that NGOs come up the curve rapidly as far as weightage to, concern for, and treatment of its human resources/ human capital are concerned.

We NGOs desperately need to take a leaf out of the corporate book – our Human Capital is at risk. Remember:

Human capital is what human capital does.
It's the invisible asset (and the biggest one) on your Balance Sheet!

Chapter IX

Compliance & Legal Risk

Once upon a time, a certain hill school had an urgent requirement for a school bus driver and so it issued advertisements in jobs sections of the national & local newspapers. The advert was answered by no less than 50 people, of whom 10 were shortlisted for interview and driving test. Here's a brief extract of the interviews of three of the shortlisted candidates.

Principal: How many years have you been driving?

Candidate A: 10 years sir.

Principal: Our school is located at the top of the hill, as you have seen on your way here. How skilled are you when it comes to driving on mountain roads?

Candidate A: Oh sir! Don't worry about that, I can drive the vehicle within two inches of the edge of the road and not go over!

Principal: Okay. Please wait outside until further instructions are given.

Principal: How many years have you been driving?

Candidate B: 12 years sir.

Principal: Our school is located at the top of the hill, as you have seen on your way here. How skilled are you when it comes to driving on mountain roads?

Candidate B: Sir, I am very skilled driver. I don't drink and drive and with my experience, I can drive the vehicle within one inch of the edge of the road and the bus won't go over the edge!

Principal: All right, thank you. Please wait outside until further instructions are given.

Principal: How many years have you been driving?

Candidate C: 15 years sir.

Principal: Our school is located at the top of the hill, as you have seen on your way here. How skilled are you when it comes to driving on mountain roads?

Candidate C: Sir, I can't say I am very skilled driver, that is for the mountain to tell you. I only know that, thanks be to God, I have not had any accidents when driving on mountain roads.

Principal: I see. Why is that?

Candidate C: No accidents, sir, because I don't drive very fast on mountain road and I keep the vehicle as far from the cliff-edge as possible.

- - - - -

It's a no-brainer which driver got the job, isn't it?

This was just a little anecdote meant to illustrate how cavalier many NGO types are when it comes to compliance with statutory & legal requirements. I have dedicated a separate chapter to this aspect of risk, because I have seen and am aware of what can happen when you run the 'gauntlet' of non-compliance with the law. Whether you don't comply out if sheer ignorance or don't comply deliberately is not the question.

A violation of the law is a violation of the law is a violation of the law!!

From Wikipedia.org, I came across the Latin version of a vital principle of law. It states '***Ignorantia juris non excusat***' and also '***ignorantia legis*** *neminem excusat'* – *meaning the principle of "Not Knowing the Law is NO defence against the law". A person who is unaware of a law may not escape liability for violating that law merely because one was unaware of its content".*

There are a great number of NGOs who unknowingly are of the opinion that since their line of work is charitable in nature, this should automatically exempt them from compliance with a number of statutory & legal provisions. In today's every evolving regulatory scenario, NGOs are subject to an equal amount of scrutiny as corporate entities, if not more.

The legal framework of the country calls for compliance under a large number of laws/acts. The crucial ones are as follows.

☞ The Employees Provident Funds and Miscellaneous Provisions Act 1952

☞ The Employees State Insurance Act 1948

☞ The Income Tax Act 1961

☞ The Payment of Gratuity Act 1972

☞ The Right of Children to Free & Compulsory Education Act 2009

☞ The Foreign Currency Regulation Act (FCRA) 2010

☞ Indian Medical Council Act 1956 (for Medical Colleges)

☞ Other laws/acts such as those relating to Land Tax/Municipal Tax/ Motor vehicles/shops and establishments, etc.

The legal framework is a minefield littered with the bones of the non-compliant! In the chapter on FCRA risks, I had mentioned how many thousands of entities had their FCRA registrations cancelled or even suspended for non-compliance with the FCRA rules.

Let's take a look at some of the laws and the penalties you will incur in event of non-compliance.

<u>**Employees Provident Funds and Miscellaneous Provisions Act 1952**</u>

Commonly referred to as the EPF or PF Act, this one is basically a welfare act which is targeted at ensuring the welfare of the employee upon retirement or job loss or welfare of the next-of-kin in case of death. The rationale was to ensure retiring employees had a lumpsum amount of money on retirement to help provide for their livelihood once they had no regular source of income. The Act provides for mandatory compliance if your organisation employs twenty or more persons. The important provisions to be noted here are as follows.

<u>Counting your twenty persons</u> (includes)

a. any person who is employed for wages in any kind of work whether that work is manual or otherwise and is in or in connection with the work of the establishment and who gets his wages directly or indirectly from the establishment/employer.

b. A person employed by or through a contractor in or in connection with the work of the establishment

c. Any person engaged as an apprentice, not being an apprentice under the Apprentices Act 1961 (52 of 1961)....

In other words, if your NGO employs 18 full-time employees and has a contractor who has provided 5 people to work there, you hit the 20 persons qualifying mark.

Calculation of PF Amount

The PF Act provided for an employee to contribute 12% of his basic <u>wages</u> plus Dearness Allowance and for the employer to contribute an equal amount. The employer also has to bear the cost of Employees Deposit Linked Insurance (EDLI) and Administrative charge, at the percentage notified from time to time (these are very small and less than 0.5%). The employer's contribution is to be sub-divided into 2 parts: 8.33% which is payable to EPS or Employees Pension Scheme and the balance 3.67% payable into Employees Provident Fund.

Since 1st Sept 2014, the threshold monthly wage limit (i.e. Basic Pay + DA) for PF calculations has been fixed at Rs. 15000.

Therefore, for an employee earning Basic + DA of Rs. 15000, the EPF contribution would be as follows.

EPF = 15000 × 12% = Rs. 1800 p.m

For the employer, the contribution for this employee EPS & EPF amounts would be as follows.

EPS = 15000 × 8.33% = Rs. 1250 (rounded off)

EPF = 15000 × 3.67% = Rs. 550 (rounded off)

Now let's take the case of an employee earning more than the Rs. 15000 (Basic + DA) threshold limit. Let us say there is an employee earning double the limit (i.e. Rs. 30000).

For the employee earning Basic + DA of Rs. 30000, the EPF contribution would be as follows.

EPF = 30000 × 12% = Rs. 3600 p.m.

For the employer, the contribution for this employee EPS & EPF amounts would be as follows.

Employer's total PF contribution on this employee would be Rs. 3600 p.m, but the breakup between EPS and EPF would be as follows.

EPS = 15000 × 8.33% = Rs. 1250 (rounded off)

EPF = Rs. 3600 minus Rs. 1250 = Rs. 2350 (rounded off)

Important Supreme Court ruling on "allowances" in PF calculation

It has been a widespread practice among corporates & other entities to break up the gross salary of an employee into various heads of pay including allowances. For example, an employee being paid a total sum of Rs. 20000 (gross salary) per month might have the following breakup.

Component of Salary	Rs.
Basic Pay	8000
Dearness Allowance (DA)	3500
HRA @ 50% (metro city)	4000
Conveyance Allowance	800
Lunch Allowance	1200
Domestic Allowance	500
Special Allowance (performance bonus/variable)	2000
Total p.m.	**20000**

Under the PF Act, the employee's Basic Pay + D.A = Rs. 11500 and his PF contribution would be Rs. 1380/-. A similar amount would be payable by the employer which would be sub-divided into EPS & EPF contribution. All very simple.

However, there were a substantial number of court cases from across the country, relating to uniformity of PF calculation methodology. Many of these cases (in appeal stage) found their way to our hon'ble Supreme Court for decision. On 28th Feb 2019, the Supreme Court made a landmark ruling defining the principles on which an allowance was to be included in basic wage for calculation of PF. It ruled that only allowances which were variable in nature or incentive linked to production/performance would be **excluded** from Basic wages, for calculation of PF.

By virtue of this definition, the employee's basic wages in the above example would shoot up to Rs. 14500. For PF calculations, adding DA, this would be Rs. 18000 and the employee's EPF contribution would be Rs. 18000 × 12% = Rs. 2160. Under the new ruling, the employee would pay Rs. 780 MORE for PF contribution and would get Rs. 780 less in net salary.

The employer, will end up paying Rs. 780 more as total PF contribution (EPS + EPF).

PF Contribution Dates & Method of Payment

Employee and employer's PF contributions must be deducted monthly and paid to EPFO within the 15th day of every month. This date is SACROSANCT – you cannot violate it. Delays in payment of PF contribution can and will result in penalties being levied on your organisation & yourself – if you are the managing director/trustee/director, etc.

The entire PF process for EPFO can be carried out online at the following web address.

https://unifiedportal.epfindia.gov.in

The payment process is as follows.

Step 1:   Calculate PF contributions (employee & employer)

Step 2:   Upload contribution details (per employee) onto EPFO website and generate TRRN (Temporary Return Reference number) and ECR (Electronic Challan cum return)

Step 3:   Generate combined challan, print combined challan & ECR for record

Step 4:   Make payment against combined challan using only online banking

Step 5:   Print payment receipt & file

PF Administration

The PF Act provided for the setup of an Employees Provident Fund Organisation (EPFO) to administer employees PF contributions from all across the country. The EPFO receives the employer & employee PF contributions, invests it, maintains records of its members (i.e. the employees of the various organisations), monitors the funds, makes payments on withdrawal requests, pays annual interest to members on their PF balances, etc. Till a few years ago, the entire EPFO system was in manual mode and excessively paper based. With the introduction of web-based applications, the entire PF system has been brought online and members can access their balances, make withdrawal requests, view the interest credited to their accounts, etc, all online. On an employee's EPFO registration (through the employer), the person is allotted an Universal Account Number (UAN) which is the member's distinct and unique PF Identification number. If the employee leaves and joins another organisation, the same UAN is applicable and a new UAN is not needed. Instead, the new employer only needs to link the UAN with a new member ID which is allotted by the new employer. For example, an employee with 5 employers in the last 15 years will be able to view details under each member ID (present and past).

For small and medium size NGOs, it is always advisable to register with EPFO and make contributions directly to EPFO, since it will be more cost effective compared to maintaining a separate PF trust for the organisation. A consultant who specialises in PF calculations and liaison with EPFO authorities can be engaged by the organisation to take care of the nitty gritty of PF work.

For very large NGOs (with a couple of thousand employees), an independent PF trust might make more sense, provided the following conditions exist.

a. You have a well laid down set of policies & procedures for PF administration (end-to-end functioning, including PF annual audit and speedy complaint resolution)

b. You have qualified staff (max. 5 persons) to handle all the documentation processes

c. You have at least ONE qualified staff to handle the investments for optimal returns as well as the documentation for investment of monies/liquidation of investments/depository operations, etc.

d. Your PF trust operates on a robust IT (information tech) backbone and is not paper based.

Penalties for PF Non-Compliance

If you comply with PF rules, good for you (i.e. your organisation & you as the leader). Don't expect any accolades from the government, because it is your duty to comply. However, if you fail to comply, the non-compliance will bring with it some major headaches to deal with. Let's take a look at some important aspects under the PF Act relating to penalties.

Section 8 of the PF Act: Mode of recovery of moneys due from employers.

This section reads as follows.

Any amount due-

(a)   from the employer in relation to an establishment to which any Scheme or the Insurance Scheme applies in respect of any contribution payable to the Fund or, as the case may be, the Insurance Fund, damages recoverable under section 14B, accumulations required to be transferred under sub-section 2 of section 15 or under sub-section 5 of section 17 or any charges payable by him under any other provision of this Act or of any provision of the Scheme or the Insurance Scheme; or

(b)   from the employer in relation to an exempted establishment in respect of any damages recoverable under section 14B or any charges payable by him the appropriate Government under any provision of this Act or under any of the conditions specified under section 17 or in respect of the contribution payable by him towards the Pension Scheme under the said section 17, may, if the amount is in arrear, be recovered in the manner specified in section 8B to 8G.

Section 8B reads as follows

8B. Issue of certificate to the Recovery Officer.

(1)   Where any amount is in arrear under Section 8, the authorised officer may issue, to the Recovery Officer, a certificate under his signature specifying the amount of arrears and the Recovery Officer, on receipt

of such certificate, shall proceed to recover the amount specified therein from the establishment or, as the case may be, the employer by one or more of the modes mentioned below:-

(a) *attachment and sale of the movable or immovable property* of the establishment or, as the case may be, the employer;

(b) *arrest of the employer and his detention in prison*;

(c) *appointing a receiver for the management of the movable or immovable properties* of the establishment or, as the case may be, the employer:

Provided that the attachment and sale of any property under this section shall first be effected against the properties of the establishment and where such attachment and sale is insufficient for recovery the whole of the amount of arrears specified in the certificate, the Recovery Officer may take such proceedings against the property of the employer for recovery of the whole or any part of such arrears.

(2) The authorised officer may issue a certificate under sub-section 1, notwithstanding that proceedings for recovery of the arrears by any other mode have been taken.

Explanation: The authorised officer of the EPFO issues a notice of recovery to the EPF Recovery Officer mentioning how much dues the defaulting organisation (establishment) has, along with relevant details. The Recovery Officer will then proceed to recover the dues from the defaulting organisation using options a, b, c, specified in section 8B – either using one option at a time or all options together. *It must be noted here that options a, b, c are not listed in order of precedence and option b can be used first by the Recovery Officer.*

To recover the PF dues of the organisation, the Recovery Officer is authorised to attach the moveable & immoveable assets/properties of the organisation AND the employer! The employer in question (defined in section 2e(i) and 2e(ii) of the PF Act) is the person who has ultimate control over the affairs of the establishment whether he/she be the managing director/director/manager/chairman, etc. In other words, you are the employer in question and your moveable & immoveable assets/properties (yes, your personal assets) can be attached and SOLD to recover PF dues. *In addition, you could also be arrested.*

Do not default on payment of your PF dues. In an absolutely worst-case scenario, if you are late by a couple of days you will be subjected to monetary penalties since the EPFO systems are computerised and can catch defaulters & delay in payments in a flash. Don't make delays a habit – simply because the software keeps track of it and the mere click of a button can throw up your entire case history in a jiffy.

Penalties for delayed PF payments

Delay time period	Penalty
Delay for up to 2 months	5% per annum
Delay from 2 months to 4 months	10% per annum
Delay from 4 months to 6 months	15% per annum
Delay in excess of 6 months	25% per annum (Could correspondingly increase to 100%)

Another piece of advice to NGOs (particularly those with financial difficulties) – your financial problems are NO EXCUSE for defaulting on PF contribution payment or delay in payment. The para below makes this crystal clear.

"The inability of an employer to make the PF contributions due to bad market conditions or defaulting customers, etc. has been held as no excuse by the Hon'ble Karnataka High Court in Chandan A. Rajan v. U.O.I & Ors. [2007 III LLJ 42]. In that case the employer was put in jail u/S. 8-B(1)(b) of the Act for failure to pay provident fund contribution though he personally narrated the facts and circumstances of his default due to market recessions, slump in the off take, his customers' default in making payment, lack of funds and mounting interest liability, and as such he was compelled to defer the statutory obligations."

(Source: http://asklabourproblem.info/civil-imprisonment-under-the-employees-provident-fund-act-miscellaneous-provisions-act-1952/)

Employee State Insurance Act 1948 (Act 34 of 1948)

Commonly referred to as the ESI Act, this one is also a welfare act/social security legislation, which is targeted at ensuring the welfare of the employee through the provision of certain benefits in case of sickness, maternity and employment injury.... etc.

Initially the phraseology of the Act provided for ESI to be applicable to factories and other establishments. It was later extended to cover educational institutions employing 20 or more persons in Rajasthan, Bihar, Pondicherry, Jammu & Kashmir, Uttarakhand, Chattisgarh, West Bengal, Jharkhand, Kerala, Uttar Pradesh, Andhra Pradesh, Assam, Punjab, Tamilnadu and to Private Medical Institutions in the State of West Bengal, Rajasthan, Bihar, Kerala, Himachal Pradesh, Uttarakhand, Andhra Pradesh, Punjab, Assam, UT Chandigarh, Jharkhand and Orissa.

ESI Benefits

The Act provides for six social security benefits, as described in section 46 of the Act.

(a) *Medical Benefit*: Full medical care is provided to an Insured person and his family members from the day he enters insurable employment, without any ceiling on expenditure on the treatment of an Insured Person or his family member.

(b) *Sickness Benefit*: Sickness Benefit is provided in the form of cash compensation at the rate of 70% of wages – payable to insured workers during the periods of certified sickness for a maximum of 91 days in a year.

(c) *Maternity Benefit*: Maternity Benefit for confinement/pregnancy is payable for Twenty Six weeks, which can be extended by one more month on medical advice.

(d) _Disablement Benefit:_ benefits for disablement such as i) Temporary disablement benefit, ii) Permanent disablement benefit and iii) Dependants Benefit are provided for.

(e) _Other Benefits:_ such as funeral expenses and confinement expenses

Treatment and hospitalisation under the ESI Act is carried out at ESI hospitals across the country and ESIC accredited medical clinics/service providers.

ESI also provides some other need-based benefits to insured workers.

Vocational Rehabilitation: To permanently disabled Insured Person for undergoing Vocational Rehab Training

Physical Rehabilitation: In case of physical disablement due to employment injury.

Old Age Medical Care: For an Insured Person retiring on attaining the age of superannuation or under VRS/ERS and for a person having to leave service due to permanent disability

Rajiv Gandhi Shramik Kalyan Yojana: Contains a scheme of Unemployment allowance for Insured Persons who become unemployed (after being insured three or more years) due to closure of factory/establishment, retrenchment or permanent invalidity.

Atal Beemit Vyakti Kalyan Yojana: providing cash compensation upto 90 days, once in a lifetime, for being rendered unemployed.

More details on each of these benefits can be obtained from https://www. esic.nic.in/information-benefits.

ESI Calculation

ESI calculation is relatively simpler than the PF calculation. ESI contribution is required to be made by both employee and employer. Till recently, the employee was required to pay a contribution equal to 1.75% of gross salary, while the employer was required to contribute an amount equal to 4.75% of the employee's gross salary.

With effect from 01.07.2019, these percentages for employee and employer contributions have been reduced to 0.75% for employee and 3.25% for employer.

The limit prescribed for ESI contribution calculation is for coverage of employees with gross salary of upto 21000 per month. Therefore, an employee with gross salary of Rs. 20000 p.m., will have the following ESI contributions,

Employee contribution = Rs. 20000 × 0.75% = Rs. 150

Employer contribution = Rs. 20000 × 3.25% = Rs. 650

ESI Contribution Dates & Method of Payment

Employee and employer's ESI contributions must be deducted monthly and paid to ESIC (Employee State Insurance Corpn.) within the 15th day of every month.

Delays in payment of ESI contribution can and will result in penalties being levied on your organisation & yourself – if you are the managing director/trustee/director, etc.

Full details on ESI Act, procedures, etc and ESIC are available at the following web address.
www.esic.nic.in

Penalties for ESI Non-Compliance

If you comply with the ESI rules, good for you and your employees because a lot of medical benefits can come their way. Over the past few years, ESIC hospitals appear to have been upgraded and offer good services to ESIC insured people.

However, if you fail to comply, the non-compliance will bring with it major headaches to deal with. Let's take a look at the important aspects under the ESI Act relating to penalties.

The below sections 85 & 85A are direct extracts from the ESI Act and are reproduced below.

85. Punishment for failure to pay contributions, etc.

If any person-

(a) fails to pay any contribution which under this Act he is liable to pay, or

(b) deducts or attempts to deduct from the wages of an employee the whole or any part of the employer's contribution, or

(c) in contravention of section 72 reduces the wages or any privileges or benefits admissible to an employee, or

(d) in contravention of section 73 or any regulation dismisses, discharges, reduces or otherwise punishes an employee, or

(e) fails or refuses to submit any return required by the regulations, or makes a false return, or

(f) obstructs any Inspector or other official of the Corporation in the discharge of his duties, or

(g) is guilty of any contravention of or non-compliance with any of the requirements of this Act or the rules or the regulations in respect of which no special penalty is provided,

He shall be punishable-

(i) where he commits an offence under clause (a), with imprisonment for a term which may extend to three years but

(a) which shall not be less than one year, in case of failure to pay the employee's contribution which has been deducted by him from the employee's wages and shall also be liable to fine of ten thousand rupees;

(b) which shall not be less than six months, in any other case and shall also be liable to fine of five thousand rupees:

PROVIDED that the Court may, for any adequate and special reasons to be recorded in the judgement, impose a sentence of imprisonment for a lesser term;

(iii) where he commits an offence under any of the clauses (b) to (g) (both inclusive), with imprisonment for a term which may extend to one year or with fine which may extend to four thousand rupees, or with both.]

85A. Enhanced punishment in certain cases after previous conviction

Whoever, having been convicted by a court of an offence punishable under this Act, commits the same offence shall, for every such subsequent offence, be punishable with imprisonment for a term which may extend to [two years and with fine of five thousand rupees]:

PROVIDED that where such subsequent offence is for failure by the employer to pay any contribution which under this Act he is liable to pay, he shall, for every such subsequent offence, be punishable with imprisonment for a term which may extend to [five years but which shall not be less than two years and shall also be liable to fine of twenty-five thousand rupees.]

85B. Power to recover damages

(1) Where an employer fails to pay the amount due in respect of any contribution or any other amount payable under this Act, the Corporation may recover [from the employer by way of penalty such damages not exceeding the amount of arrears as may be specified in the regulations]:

PROVIDED that before recovering such damages, the employer shall be given a reasonable opportunity of being heard

While the above clauses would seem straightforward to anyone with a knowledge of legalese, let me decrypt the above for you.

☞ If you have deducted the ESI contribution from an employee and failed to pay it to ESIC, as per section 85(i)(a) you can be jailed for upto 3 (Three) years but definitely not less than one year, as well as fined Rs. 10000 (Rupees Ten thousand).

☞ If you have **not** deducted the ESI contribution from an employee and no contribution has been made at all to ESIC, as per section 85(i)(b) you can be jailed for upto 3 (Three) years but definitely not less than six months, as well as fined Rs. 5000 (Rupees Five thousand).

☞ For violations listed under section 85, sub-sections (b) to (g), such as deducting/attempting to deduct the employer's ESI contribution from the employee's salary OR reduce employee wages against the provisions of section 72 OR dismiss/punish an employee during period of sickness (section 73) OR fail/refuse to submit ESI return or submit false return OR obstruct an ESI inspector/officer from carrying out his duties OR non-compliance with any provisions of the ESI Act; then as per section 85(ii) you can be jailed for upto 1 (One) year or be fined upto Rs. 4000 (Rupees Four thousand) – or you could be jailed & fined.

☞ Section 85A states that if you have been convicted by a court of law for an offence under the ESI Act and you commit the same offence again, for every such subsequent offence, you could be punished by being jailed for upto two years and with fine of five thousand rupees.

☞ Section 85B states that if an employer fails to pay the amount due in respect of any contribution or any other amount payable under the ESI Act, the ESIC may recover damages/penalties which may extend to as much as the amount of arrears (amount due for payment).

☞ Delay in payment of ESI dues can attract a penalty of 12% per annum.

Please do not take ESI contributions (deduction & payment) lightly. It can prove financially disastrous in the future. I happen to know of an organisation which defaulted on ESI payments for months and ended up with past payments being due, as well as a massive penalty slapped on them almost equal to the arrears. Therefore, under similar conditions (hypothetically) if you had ESI dues of INR 3 million (Rs. 30 lakhs) for 6 months, with the penalties slapped, your total ESI liability could become INR 6 million (Rs. 60 lakhs). It can only be described as financial "hara-kiri" (ritual suicide by disembowelment by a sword)!

The Payment of Gratuity Act, 1972 (No. 39 of 1972)

In August 1972, an Act was passed by Parliament called The Payment of Gratuity Act, 1972 which provided a scheme by which gratuity was to be paid to employees.

Why gratuity and what is it? If we take a look at the meaning of the word 'gratuity', it evolved from old French or Latin, circa late 15th century and generally meant graciousness or favour. The origin in Old French lay in the word '*gratuité*' or in medieval Latin in the word '*gratuitas*' or gift, again from the Latin word '*gratus*' which meant pleasing or thankful. Gratuity is essentially a gift payable by an employer to an employee as a monetary thank you to the employee for many years of service. Prior to the Gratuity Act of 1972, such monetary thank you would have been more the exception than the rule, depending solely on the graciousness & largesse of the employer. The Gratuity Act made payment of gratuity compulsory. It is meant to be a reward for long-service to an employer. It is payable to the employee on retirement/resignation or termination or to his nominees in case of death.

Applicability – The Gratuity Act applies to factories, mines, oilfields, plantations, ports and railway company, shops or establishments, such other establishments or class of establishments, in which ten or more employees are employed. It therefore applies to NGOs, educational institutions, hospitals, etc. It is important to note here that if you had ten (10) or more employees on any DAY of the preceding twelve months, then you are liable to pay Gratuity as per the terms of the Act. Even if the number of employees drops below ten in subsequent years, you are still liable to pay gratuity.

Nomination – An employee who has completed one year of service needs to fill in and provide to the employer a gratuity nomination form. This form tells the employer whom to make the gratuity payment to in case of death of the employee.

Section 6(3) of the Act states that if an employee has a family at the time of making a nomination, then the nomination shall be made only in favour of one or more members of the family and any earlier nomination already made in favour of any other person (non-family member) shall become void.

Section 6(4) however, states if at the time of making a nomination, the employee has no family, the nomination may be made in favour of any person or persons. If the employee subsequently, acquires a family, then the nomination already made shall become invalid and the employee has to submit a fresh nomination (within ninety days from the date of acquiring a family), nominating one or more members of his family.

Continuous service – The Gratuity Act provides for something called 'continuous service' in section 2A, which is a term that requires clear understanding as this is an area often misunderstood.

2A. Continuous Service.- (1) For the purpose of this Act-
(1) An employee shall be said to be in continuous service for a period if he has, for that period, been in uninterrupted service, including service which may be interrupted on account of sickness, accident, leave, absence from duty without leave (not being absence in respect of which an order treating the absence as break in service has been passed in accordance with the standing orders, rules or regulations governing the employees of the establishment), lay-off, strike or a lock-out or cessation of work not due to any fault of the employee, whether such uninterrupted or interrupted service was rendered before or after the commencement of this Act;

An employee is therefore said to have been in continuous service for a time period which includes interruptions on account of sickness, leave, absence from work without leave, being laid-off, strike, lock-out or cessation of work – such that these interruptions *are not due to the fault of the employee.* If any absence from work without leave is not treated as a break-in-service (as per the rules & regulations of the organisation), then such leave becomes part of uninterrupted service. However, if as per organisation rules, such leave is declared or constitutes a break in service then the period of continuous service ends when the unsanctioned (or absence without leave) leave begins.

Let's look at an illustration to better understand this. An employee has worked for 15 years availing of annual leaves, occasional sick leave days, casual leave, etc. In the 16th year of service the employee has a heart attack and is hospitalised for 2 months. On the 61st day he returns to work and resigns from work with immediate effect (say 15.10.2019) being unable to continue working on account of his heart condition. For the purpose of gratuity calculation, his period of continuous service would be upto the last date of service would be 15.10.2019 – including the period of sickness/hospitalisation. I am aware of at least one organisation which has completely misunderstood section 2A or not given due cognizance to its contents possibly out of sheer ignorance.

Calculation of gratuity – The gratuity calculation formula is rather simple, once you have the number of years of continuous service worked out. The factors to consider are as follows before the actual calculation can be made.

- ☞ Ascertain date of joining (DoJ) & last date of service.
- ☞ Calculate the number of years & months of service from DoJ to last date of service. Take care to ensure there is no break in service of the employee. An employee who has been working on temporary basis for 6 months or on a one year contract followed by a break in service (could be 7 days or more), such temporary service/contract period would not count as part of 'continuous service'.
- ☞ Check for 5 years continuous service – To be eligible for gratuity, an employee needs to have 5 (five) years continuous service. Check if this condition is fulfilled, (Section 4 of the Gratuity Act)
- ☞ Round off the years of service – if an employee ha worked for 7 years 7 months, the years of service need to be rounded off to 8 years. In case of 7 years 5 months, this would be rounded off to 7 years. This is to be done because section 4(2) of the Act provides for the payment of gratuity for every "completed year of service or part thereof in excess of 6 months…"

☞ Ascertain Basic + DA – Obtain from the employee's salary calculation/ salary sheet, the last drawn Basic pay & Dearness Allowance (on full month basis).

☞ Gratuity calculation as follows.

Gratuity formula = No of years of service (rounded off) × 15/26 × (Basic + DA)

Gratuity eligibility by Supreme Court – Most of us tend to use the 'five years continuous service' as a sacrosanct benchmark for calculation of gratuity eligibility – even a day less than 5 years being interpreted as not eligible. Section 2(a)(ii) of the Act however provides otherwise.

In a Supreme Court case of Surendra Kumar Verma vs. Central Govt. Industrial Tribunal, the Hon'ble Supreme Court ruled that it is enough that an employee has a service of 240 days in the preceding 12 months and it is not necessary that the employee should have completed one whole year's service. This was the definition of continuous service applied by the Hon'ble Supreme court in an Industrial Dispute Act case and since the words 'continuous service' are applicable in the Payment of Gratuity Act, the same principle can be adopted under the Gratuity act also.

An employee who has therefore worked (in continuous service) for a period of 4 years 240 days is therefore automatically eligible for gratuity – with a deemed service period of 5 years.

Employers are advised to take special note of this, as an employee eligible for gratuity under this rule/principle might be denied gratuity and then you might find yourself hauled before the Controlling Authority/the High Court/ Supreme Court for denial to pay gratuity as per the provisions of the Act.

Payment due date & mode of payment – Section 7(3) of the Gratuity Act states that "The employer shall arrange to pay the amount of gratuity within thirty days from the date it becomes payable to the person to whom the gratuity is payable."

You have 30 days to pay gratuity from the employee's last date of service (provided all exit formalities are complied with).

Employers please take special note of this clause of the Gratuity Act. If you fail to pay gratuity in 30 days you become liable for the penalty under section 7(3A) provided below.

While the Payment of Gratuity Rules provide for payment of gratuity in cash or by DD/cheque as per the choice of the payee (beneficiary), it is this author's opinion/recommendation that you pay gratuity to the employee/nominee by way of cheque (or demand draft/pay order) obtaining a receipt/declaration from the employee/nominee of having received the gratuity cheque. This is the best way of obtaining solid documentation. However, when paying by cheque please ensure you have sufficient funds to clear the cheque. A gratuity cheque bouncing can become grounds for delay in payment of gratuity/fraud. An alternate means of payment would be by RTGS/NEFT but employee/nominee signature for receipt of gratuity must be obtained before funds can be transferred and employee/nominee may not agree to provide this before payment is received.

Penalties

Now we come to the penalties under the Gratuity Act or what I would prefer to call the 'risk' section. Non-compliance with the provisions of the Act, carries with the following penalties.

Section 7(3A): Delayed payment of gratuity: This section states

"If the amount of gratuity payable under sub-section (3) is not paid by the employer within the period specified in sub-section (3) the employer shall pay, from the date on which the gratuity becomes payable to the date on which it is paid, simple interest at such rate, not exceeding the rate notified by the Central Government from time to time for repayment of long term deposits, as that Government may, by notification specify…

Provided that no such interest shall be payable if the delay in the payment is due to the fault of the employee and the employer has obtained permission in writing from the Controlling Authority for the delayed payment on this ground]."

Under the sub-heading 'payment due date' I had mentioned that gratuity needs to be paid within 30 days from the date it becomes payable. Delay beyond 30 days attracts penalty interest under Section 7(3A) and is payable @ 10% p.a. on simple interest basis. Therefore, if an employee's gratuity of say Rs. 5 lakhs is due for the past 1 year, as the employer you become liable to pay an additional sum of Rs. 50000 as penal interest to the employee. Your gratuity liability therefore becomes Rs. 550,000 after one year. Don't play games with timely gratuity payment – you will only end up digging your grave and the organisation's financial grave deeper!

Section 9 Penalties

Section 9(1) Whoever, for the purpose of avoiding any payment to be made by himself under this Act or of enabling any other person to avoid such payment, knowingly makes or causes to be made any false statement or false representation shall be punishable with imprisonment for a term which may extend to six months, or with fine which may extend to ten thousand rupees or with both.

Explanation: Be careful of the statements made by you or your representative on gratuity. Do not issue false statements to avoid payment, as these may be recorded and submitted in a court of law, earning you a jail term or fine or both.

Section 9(2) An employer who contravenes, or makes default in complying with, any of the provisions of this Act or any rule or order made thereunder shall be punishable with imprisonment for a term [which shall not be less than three months but which may extend to one year, or with fine which shall not be less than ten thousand rupees but which may extend to twenty thousand rupees, or with both]:

Provided that where the offence relates to non-payment of any gratuity payable under this Act, the employer shall be punishable with imprisonment, for a term which shall not be less than [six months but which may extend to two years] unless the Court trying the offence, for reasons to be recorded by it in writing, is of opinion that a lesser term of imprisonment or the imposition of a fine would meet the ends of justice.

Explanation: Under section 9(2) if you do not comply with the provisions of the Gratuity Act, you can be jailed for 3 months upto one year or fined between Rs. 10000 to Rs. 20000 or both jailed & fined.

However, if the non-compliance relates to 'non-payment of any gratuity payable under this Act' then as the employer you could be jailed for between six months to two years, unless the Court trying the offence feels otherwise and gives a lesser jail term or imposes a fine.

Death case gratuity payment & documentation: In case of death of an employee, the prescribed term of 5 years continuous service clause does not hold good. Gratuity will be calculated on number of years of completed service. An employee dying after 3 years in service, gratuity for the 3 years' service will be paid to the nominee. However, if an employee has served for more than 5 years continuous service the standard gratuity calculation formula applies.

As far as death case documentation is concerned, the employer must obtain at least the following (strongly recommended by this author).

a. *Death certificate copy* – issued by Municipal Corporation/Panchayat/ etc. Verify this with the original & provide a certification on the photocopy copy that it has been verified with the original. Retain the copy and return the original.

b. *Nomination form in original* – This has to be on file/in safe custody with the employer from before. *It cannot be submitted by nominees after the employee's death.* In the absence of a nomination form, ask the next of kin to obtain succession certificate from a court of law (issued by First Class Judicial Magistrate). Do not take a decision on who should be paid the gratuity.

c. *ID & address proof of nominee/s* – This is crucial for you to know whether the nominee presenting himself of herself is the actual person or not. Verify the copies with originals and certify the fact on the copies. For spouse/children of the deceased, you can verify the employee's name as spouse or father of the nominee/s. This is an added precaution. Also obtain their bank details including proof of spelling, etc so that gratuity payment cheque is issued in correct name or RTGS/NEFT is sent correctly.

d. *Affidavits/indemnities* as necessary – To protect the organisation from potential risks in case of discrepancies in documents, etc, you may obtain sworn affidavits/indemnities from the nominees. It is advisable to consult your lawyer for these.

- - - - -

One of the biggest problems you will face as the 'employer' in an NGO, is the funds constraint, for complying with gratuity/PF/ESI payments. The reason for this is simple – most donors do not factor in or provide for administrative costs (read as salaries + labour law compliance costs) when they make their donations/commitments. The donor expects that 100% of his/her donation will be utilised for the betterment of the beneficiary. Post the Wall Street crash of 2008 and the consequent recessionary period, every donor has become that much more cost conscious as far as their money is concerned. They want 'more bang for the buck'.

However, as an entity, if you do not comply with the labour laws of the country you can and will be subject to either very serious litigation and financial penalties or worse – imprisonment. With the government's information systems moving to a level where different departmental software talk to/interface with each other, you can be sure that an infringement/non-compliance on PF may become visible to an inspector for ESI in case of a non-compliance on ESI, etc. You will suddenly find you have 'nowhere to run and nowhere to hide' – to the entire statutory establishment you are a 'serial, chronic defaulter' and no amount of begging or pleading will reduce your punishment.

Therefore, at the time of raising funds clearly mention to donors & well-wishers what percentage of their donation goes into meeting administrative costs including salaries & statutory compliance costs. Let your donor know because he/she clearly understands that without the people to do the work, nothing will reach the beneficiary. How does one impart vocational skills training to poor students without teachers?

The backbone of each and every NGO is its people who ensure that 'last-mile delivery' of the objective/s. Also be transparent and build the staff costs including labour-law compliance costs into your budgets – do not try to hide these. It will help you to know the exact cost of delivering a particular service/benefit to the beneficiary.

Compliance with Miscellaneous Laws/Acts

The PF Act, ESI Act & Gratuity Act are the important acts with which almost all NGOs have to comply. There are a number of other laws for which compliance is also necessary but for the sake of brevity, I will not dwell on these in detail.

Profession Tax: Profession Tax is a tax levied and collected by the respective state government. It applies to any person earning an income from salary or anyone practicing a profession such as chartered accountant, company secretary, lawyer, doctor etc. The Profession Tax Act is primarily a State legislation subject – a power granted to the respective state governments by way of Article 276 of the Constitution of India 1949. Each state has the right to define the rate of taxation per salary slab/per income slab per profession. Different states provide for different rates.

Commonly referred to as PTax, this amount is deductible from the monthly wages/salary of the employee and is payable into the treasury of the respective state government (or to the state govt. where the head office of the organisation is located). PTax is NOT an employer expense but an employee expense, though the compliance responsibility rests with the employer. Having stated this, a finance professional such as myself finds it incomprehensible as to how an organisation chooses to ignore the responsibility of PTax compliance. Though the penalties are not as severe/high as some other labour legislation/ tax laws, the only problem an organisation & it's leadership should have with PTax, is the cost of compliance (i.e. engaging a consultant/full time or part time employee to compute the employee-wise PTax, remit the same to the state government and file the PTax returns). Some NGOs would rather risk the wrath of the state government than bear the minimal cost of compliance.

Minimum Wages Act: In order to bring about standardisation in the wage level in our country, the concept of minimum wages was introduced after Independence. The Minimum Wages Act 1948 categorised workers into 3 categories (skilled, semi-skilled & unskilled) across a broad categorisation of job types. Under the Act the minimum wage per day across the country is defined, by the Central Govt., from time to time. Since wages differ across the country based on demand & supply of labour from state to state, the respective state govts., define the minimum wage levels in each state. The minimum wage level in any state, however, cannot be lower than the minimum wage per day defined by the central govt. The stage govt., can notify changes in the state's minimum wages per category/job type on bi-annual/annual basis, etc. It is vital to keep checking the state govt. labour department's website every quarter or every six months to ensure staying upto date on minimum wage notifications and compliance.

The relevance of this act for the NGO lies in compliance with the salary/ wage levels adhered to for the employees of the NGO. If the state govt., provides for a minimum wage of Rs. 7500 p.m. for an 'unskilled' security guard, we (the NGO) cannot be found to be paying Rs. 7000 p.m., or even Rs. 7250 p.m. to a security guard. While the Act prescribes penalties for non-compliance, the more immediate 'penalty' for payment of a lower-than-minimum-wage, would be labour unrest, political repercussions (read agitations) and even earning the 'displeasure' of the state govt.

Motor Vehicles Act: Most NGOs possess at least one vehicle (whether motorbike or scooter or car, etc) for travel/conveyance purposes, whether intra-city or inter-city. Along with the ownership/possession of a vehicle comes the need for compliance with the Motor Vehicles Act. Registration of a vehicle, drivers' licence and its validity, updated Pollution-under-control (PUC) certificate, vehicle road-worthiness, responsible driving, etc are all aspects which need consideration and compliance. Non-compliance brings with it risks which are measurable largely in terms of fines and with the recent amendment to the Motor Vehicles Act in 2019, stiff fines can be imposed for various infringements under the Act. The cost of non-compliance has therefore sky-rocketed under the Act and the risk (financial) has multiplied exponentially.

Right of Children to Free & Compulsory Education Act (2009): Many NGOs are into the field of education either through the running of schools, vocational skill centres, colleges or even medical education. For those running schools, this Act (commonly known as the RTE Act) has particular relevance. The broad features of the Act are as follows.

☞ It covers children (male & female) of the ages six (6) to fourteen (14) years

☞ It covers elementary education or education from Class I to Class 8.

☞ School means any recognised school imparting elementary education, including a school receiving Govt. grants or local authority grants as well as 'unaided' schools.

☞ Section 3(1) of the Act states that every child of age 6 to 14 years shall have the right to free and compulsory education in a neighbourhood school, till completion of elementary education.

☞ Section 3(2) goes on to state that no child (mentioned in sec 3(1)) shall be liable to pay a kind of fee/charges/expenses which may prevent the child from pursuing/completing elementary education.

☞ 25% seats in private schools are to be reserved for RTE students.

☞ Section 13(2b) of the Act does away with screening procedure for children/parents, making this a punishable offence.

☞ Section 16 clearly states that no child admitted in a school shall be held back in any class or expelled from school till the completion of elementary education.

☞ Section 17(1) states that no child shall be subjected to physical punishment or mental harassment.

☞ Section 21 of the Act provides for the constitution of a School Management Committee (SMC) which will comprise of elected representatives of local authority, parents/guardians of the school children & teachers. 50% of the SMC members must be women and 75% of the SMC members must be parents/guardians of children admitted in the school. The SMC shall monitor the working of the school, prepare recommend school development plan and monitor the utilisation of govt grants/local authority grants.

☞ The RTE Act provides for a minimum Pupil-Teacher Ratio (one teacher for every 30 students from Class I to Class V and one teacher for every 35 students from Class VI to Class VIII)

☞ Section 28 is crystal clear in stating that no teacher shall engage in private tuition or private teaching activity.

☞ There should be at least one specialised teacher each for (i) Science & Mathematics (ii) Social Studies and (iii) Languages

☞ The schedule to the Act provides for certain minimum requirements for building/academic instructional hours, teachers working hours, library, etc. Some of these are listed below.

   a. At least one class-room for every teacher

   b. Office-cum-store-cum head Teacher's room

   c. Separate toilets for boys and girls

   d. Safe & adequate drinking water facility for all children

   e. Kitchen where mid-day meal is cooked

   f. Playground

   g. Boundary wall/fencing to secure the school building

h. Minimum working days (200 days and 800 instruction hours for Class I to Class V/220 days and 1000 instruction hours for Class VI to Class VIII)

i. Minimum 45 working hours per week per teacher, including preparation time

j. There must be a library in each school which provides newspapers, magazines, books on all subjects including story-books.

☞ The Central Govt & State Govt., will jointly share the responsibility for providing funds for RTE. Expenditure by unaided schools on providing free & compulsory education under RTE (i.e. the 25% seats) shall be reimbursed upto a) per child expenditure incurred by the State or b) actual expenditure charged from the child – whichever is LESS.

RTE Act as applicable to Minority institutions –

Our country has many schools and educational institutes run by what are known as 'minorities'. After the RTE Act 2009 came into existence, the major question/confusion which arose was whether the RTE Act applied to all schools including those established & administered by minorities. Article 30 of the Indian Constitution provides certain rights to the minorities of our country.

Article 30 of the Constitution of India 1949 states:

30. Right of minorities to establish and administer educational institutions

(1) All minorities, whether based on religion or language, shall have the right to establish and administer educational institutions of their choice

(1A) In making any law providing for the compulsory acquisition of any property of an educational institution established and administered by a minority, referred to in clause (1), the State shall ensure that the amount fixed by or determined under such law for the acquisition of such property is such as would not restrict or abrogate the right guaranteed under that clause

(2) The state shall not, in granting aid to educational institutions, discriminate against any educational institution on the ground that it is under the management of a minority, whether based on religion or language

The mere statement of Article 30(1) seems to answer the question, though not entirely.

In an important Supreme Court case ruling (Pramati Educational & Cultural Trust v. Union of India, (2014) 8 SCC 1), the Hon'ble Court ruled as follows on the RTE Act -

"….But insofar as the RTE Act applies to minority schools, aided or unaided, it offends Art. 30(1) and is ultra vires the Constitution…"
Source: www.supremecourtcases.com (http://www.supremecourtcases.com/index2.php?option=com content&itemid=99999999&do pdf=1&id=46136)

From this ruling, it is adequately clear that the RTE Act of 2009 cannot supersede the Constitution of India and therefore, the RTE Act does not hold good for minority schools. However, a subsequent ruling, in WP(C).No. 30712 of 2015 in the Kerala High Court case of Sobha George v State of Kerala, provided an important insight and applicability of the RTE Act 2009 to minority institutions.

The Kerala High Court ruled in Point 27 of its' judgement in respect of Article 30(1) s applicable to different sections of the RTE Act: (reproduced verbatim – source: https://indiankanoon.org/doc/123893874/) (italics introduced by this author for emphasis on key aspects)

27. Next point to be examined is; what is the extent of right that could be claimed by a minority educational institution in relation to the fundamental right claimed by a child. Article 30 (1) of the Constitution protects the rights of the minorities to establish and administer educational institution of their choice. This is essentially a right to

create a feeling of security among minorities and a declaration that they will be treated at par with the majority in all respects. *Minority institutions have no superior right that can be claimed by them in terms of the Constitution to deny rights of others.* The right, as guaranteed under Article 30(1), is to protect the mere right to retain the character of the distinct nature of the culture, social identity, etc. of the minority status. *Thus, the special provision is provided to permit them to establish and administer institution such that it retains its identity and character.*

No minority can be heard to say that to protect their identity, they have a right to trample upon the rights of others which are asserted or claimed not in derogation of goals of Article 30(1) of the Constitution. No right of minority will be affected if a child is ordered to be promoted to a higher level class. As has been noted, protection as envisaged under the Constitution is to protect the minority character of the educational institution. Therefore, when denial of others' rights by such institutions have no nexus or relation with the object of the protection, court has to denounce upon such claim.

And again later, in the same point 27:

"The right to administer is said to consist of four principal matters. First is the right to choose its managing or governing body. Second is the right to choose its teachers. Third is the right not to be compelled to refuse admission to students. Fourth is the right to use its properties and assets for the benefit of its own institutions."

Therefore, from the above case, it can be seen while Article 30(1) of the Constitution allows minority schools to remain outside the purview of the RTE Act 2009, there are provisions in the RTE Act which provide certain right to others (i.e. children). The provisions of Article 30(1) cannot trample on the rights of others, including the rights of children. The RTE Act of 2009 provides for a number of items which are beneficial to the right to life of children – items which cannot be seen as detrimental or harmful to the rights of minorities or their identity or character. Therefore, such provisions of the RTE Act 2009 should be upheld and implemented by minority schools (such as student-teacher ratio, provisions relating to teaching hours/days, building, library, separate toilets, etc).

An excellent piece of reading in this regard would be Ajey Sangai's article 'Harmonising RTE with minority schools' published in The Hindu (https://www.thehindu.com/opinion/op-ed/Harmonising-RTE-with-minority-schools/article14472702.ece),

- - - - -

Conclusion: This has been a rather long and arduous (though not exhaustive) look at compliance with the various laws of the land. In the absence of compliance with the law, we are no better than the corporate defaulter and *our NGO status is no badge-of-exemption*. It is important, as NGOs, that we get our legal compliance bit correct and then some. Without this, we are just a bunch of wannabe do-gooders driving very close to the edge, and we all know what happens to drivers who drive close to the edge – sooner or later.

'Ignorantia juris non excusat'
'Ignorantia legis neminem excusat'

Chapter X

Leadership Risk

Hundreds and thousands of books have been penned by various authors on the concept of 'Leadership' – a subject that forms the very basis of management, corporate practice, seminars, conferences, consultancy, leadership habits, et al – a topic that has spawned a veritable industry of its own.

Indeed, leadership is a very crucial and integral part of every form of organisation – be it corporate, social, political, government, financial, etc. Each of the entities employing people has to have one or more leaders. The corporate cannot function without a leader to interpret the vision and provide strategy and direction. The same goes for the social sector organisation and the political party. Even government cannot function without a President or Prime Minister or Chancellor to lead the government.

The role of leadership is as the name suggests – 'to lead'. Leaders lead others in the efforts and attempts at achievement of a goal or a set of goals. The leader of any (form of) organisation is much like the pilot or the driver who guides the vehicle (i.e. the organisation) to its destination (objective). He or she is the 'lynch-pin' for the organisation – the one who holds it all together.

The absence of leadership results in a void, which spawns chaos, anarchy, drift and even organisational decline. What is an army without a General to lead it? Nothing but a bunch of rabble rousers, good for nothings.

However, that's not the subject matter of this chapter – we will not be dwelling on the absence of leadership. Instead we will take a look at the risk that the <u>presence</u> of certain types of leadership & leadership qualities, primarily in the context of the NGO.

Can leadership be deemed a risk-factor? Indeed.

To understand the risks that leadership (and leaders) pose to the NGO, one must first understand certain aspects of leadership and the very crux of leadership.

Understanding the Mantle of Control

The first and foremost thing we need to do is to understand the 'MANTLE OF CONTROL'. In olden times (and even now in family businesses), the transfer of power and responsibility from father to son, from reigning incumbent or king to crown prince or lord, was by the placing of the incumbent's mantle or cloak on the successor's shoulders. In Roman & Greek worlds it was sometimes symbolized by the handing down of the family ring or seal of authority. In Biblical times, the mantle was placed on the next man's shoulders, as Elijah the prophet did with Elisha – his successor.

The passing on of the mantle or ring, was not the mere passing of power but the passing of *tremendous responsibility*. Along <u>with that responsibility went the authority, which was required to carry out the tremendous responsibility placed upon the inheritor's shoulders.</u> It must be noted that THE RESPONSIBILITY CAME FIRST, the authority came later.

The problem with the passing of the mantle of control today, is that we leaders take the mantle of control to symbolize the attainment of power and authority thereby forsaking (read as ignoring or trivialising) the responsibility. As the leader, I have now become like God, in my own little world. We see the authority first and become so blinded by it that we forget that there is a massive responsibility too. Then we try to run the kingdom (read 'organisation') based on authority alone. Far too many of us take this mantle of control too lightly, many others don't even know it exists. A promotion to a leadership position just means more money, more perks, more control, more power, a company

car, an expense account, bigger bonuses, more people below us to pick on ......
and so on.

As I said earlier, the mantle of control means the responsibility has been placed on our shoulders first, the authority comes later. It has been placed upon OUR shoulders, because we have been thought to be capable of *wisely and judiciously* leading our organizations ahead into the future. We have been weighed on the scales and considered capable of shouldering the responsibility that goes with the higher position. We often look at it with a bottom-up view as 'the responsibility goes with the position'. Not so, my friend. *It is the position which goes with the responsibility!!*

What one must also understand is that when the mantle of control is placed on your shoulders, that mantle is NOT placed on you because you are the ONLY one for the job or because you are the best man for it.

The reality is you are 'considered' to be the best person AVAILABLE at the moment, because *someone better was not available at the time*. Know that - **the 'someone' better than you, does exist** – in fact many better people exist, when compared to you. It's just that since they were not available at the time, the job was given to you. When a job advert is issued, placement consultants and head-hunters scour the globe/nation for suitable candidates. Along comes a sheaf of Curriculum Vitae of a million and one candidates (not the case for NGOs though, as a few dozen or more CVs would come). Yet, if even one potential candidate is not on that list, the recruiter has not been accorded 'unbridled universal' choice – his choice amounts to 'limited choice'. The recruiter can only choose from the applications received and the candidates interviewed – his ability to get the best man for the job is constricted. The best man may still be out there somewhere and the one selected is therefore not the best. Many of us have been placed in our positions of leadership across the globe by such consultants and head-hunters, but there was always at least one better person missing from the 'pond of fish' – since he or she was not available at the time. Therefore, the biggest shark in the pond will still be a 'small fry' in the ocean.

Never think that we are the best, there is always someone better. When we think we are the best, we begin to think we are immortal and irreplaceable and more importantly – we think we are 'god'.

Since there is always a bigger fish out there, bigger than you – you are therefore replaceable – NOT IRREPLACEABLE. The moment you begin to think that you are the only/most perfect man for the job, that's the time you become the most imperfect or the worst man for the job. Therefore, as a leader we are merely the CUSTODIANS of a great responsibility and must exercise our control judiciously.

Quite often, leaders of NGOs tend to think they are the 'cat's whiskers' and no-one better than them exists. The basis for such thinking lies in the fact that the pond for their leadership tends to be small, as compared to the corporate, and hence the mistaken belief in being irreplaceable.

Truth be told, responsibility in the NGO is even greater than the corporate. While corporates focus on business goals and making money, the social sector organisation's focus is primarily on delivering help/assistance to underprivileged society – that which government and corporate have not been able to. NGOs are by and large the crucial safety net that the underprivileged have. The corporate leader shirking responsibility will result in the loss of a few millions. The NGO leader driving in the wrong direction can wreck the only chance the underprivileged might have at a better life – a lost opportunity on which value cannot be placed. In the NGO, leadership is more about the responsibility than the authority.

This misconceived premise of authority-first-responsibility-later, is therefore what I would call the 'Leadership Authority Risk factor' – the self-belief that it is all about me and my authority. No knowledge of or concern for the mantle of control and the responsibility it carries. More often than not, the Leadership Authority Risk combines with what I call the 'Leadership Ego' (it's all about me) presenting a very deadly visage as the face of the organisation/department.

The NGO leader's foundation stone of authority and power instead of one of over-whelming responsibility coupled with authority presents a very serious leadership risk to the social sector.

The 'Greater-than-thou' risk

Many leaders and CEOs, upon occupying the corner office, cut themselves off from their people – becoming typical bosses or overlords. Never make this mistake – be it corporate and more particularly NGO.

When you separate yourself from your team, you create a schism in the organization, you begin the evolution of a setup called the 'we & them hierarchy'. This process of separation is something, which comes naturally to all of us – the rising above the crowd and then looking down upon them and regarding them as the backward classes of our own world. Most of the time, we do this totally unintentionally, without meaning to exert our position over others, it's just that our positions get to our heads.

The truth is, we also come from the ranks of those same 'backward classes' we look down upon. We were once junior managers, custodians, clerks, ordinary salesmen, counter-workers, data entry operators, frontline employees and so on. Once upon a time – not so long ago – we rubbed shoulders with the people we now look down upon. So why should we be or behave so different from them, once we take a step up the ladder of hierarchy?

"Oh, but the employees who work for me (oops, sorry, correction), who work _with_ me, will begin to take me for granted and will never listen to what I have to say."

As a boss, we need to balance the requirement of being a boss and getting things done, with the requirement of being a friend and colleague and carrying people along with us.

This is all about efficiency. More effort goes into hauling, tugging and pushing a heavy load to its destination than the effort which goes into putting the load on a cart with wheels and pulling the cart. The objectives in an organization can be achieved by using the whip or by collective participation. These are the two extremes of the spectrum – the best position would be a balance of the two. One generates a lot of friction and grumbling while the other tends to cause things to work more smoothly. The use of the whip typically represents the 'Greater than thou' school of thought and its consequent risk of slowing achievement down in the medium to long run.

When you do this, people view you as the boss – and the boss is always wrong and is therefore always regarded as the enemy. Nobody co-operates readily with the enemy, except the skunks.

It is a fact that people must know, understand and accept that you are the boss, else they would never listen when you issue orders. They must know that as the boss, you have powers and a whip in your hand for use, but they must also know that that whip will be used judiciously and wisely. People must also know and understand that you are one of them – a part of the team. The only difference between them and you, is the title and the authority and responsibility. You lead them but are still a part of them.

Being a 100% boss will see your NGO function on the lines of a dictatorship with little or no participation from the team.

In today's dynamic world settings with ever changing rules and regulations for NGOs, leaders are bound to miss something that their team members (or one-downs) may notice. Being a dictator stifles and kills participation from the team.

The 'I-Know-It-All' Risk

Another very critical mistake we leaders make is to think that we are always right, we know it all and the team consists of a bunch of ignoramuses (or idiots). Since we have attained the level above others, it means that we are of superior knowledge than others and therefore we have all the answers. This tends to heighten our belief in ourselves as supreme and all knowing. As a leader, understand that none of us has all the answers.

Let's understand that **we do not have all the answers.** It is necessary for us to also depend on those around us and who work with us – particularly in support roles. Most of the time, these people are the ones who have answers that we may not have and may know what to do. The moment we accept & admit that we don't have all the answers (i.e. we are not super-computers), is the time when our egos take a backseat and take a little deflating – directly reducing the 'I-know-it-all' risk as well as the 'Leadership Authority' risk.

The result of taking assistance from someone else is two-fold – the other person feels good that they have been consulted and *you have learnt something new*!!

I know a leader with the classic flaw-hubris of 'I-know-it-all' and went as far as enforcing his opinion on all and sundry including advisors and even consultants. (The world over consultants are widely acknowledged as people who are considered experts in their fields or possessing a substantial expertise on a subject).

If we don't know something, let's admit we don't and let's learn it instead. Rather than admit our own ignorance, we prefer to adopt the wrong path and often end up miles from our destination.

So, stop thinking you are right and everyone else is wrong! Don't risk it, the NGO will suffer for your 'I-know-it-all' risk.

'Micro-management' risk

A downstream risk of the 'I-know-it-all' risk is the 'micro-management risk'. A leader who thinks he or she knows it all also thinks others in the team know nothing and can do nothing, let alone do it efficiently.

They begin to micro-manage everything – checking every full-stop, every comma, double checking every word. Such behaviour undermines the confidence of the one-downs. Skilled one-downs become demotivated and leave, directly impacting the NGO through Human Capital risk.

Additionally, micro-management results in inefficiency and time wasted on micro matters at a leader's level. Time wasted – which could be more effectively employed in defining strategy for the NGO and improving the delivery mechanisms.

The 'Cerberus-leadership' risk

Picture with me Cerberus or the Greek mythological 'hound of Hades' which had three heads, one body, a snake for a tail and whose capture was one of the twelve labours of Hercules.

In Greek mythology Cerberus was a fearsome, dangerous beast. In management too, a Cerberus leader is a dangerous managerial creature and a ridiculous one too. Unfortunately, I have found the existence of such a creature in NGO management spheres too – with disastrous results.

Can you imagine a department with THREE heads and one deputy head? One named 'Finance Head X', a second 'Finance Head Y', and 'Additional Finance Head' and then a 'Deputy Finance Head'. The million-dollar question that begs askance here is: who is the actual dept. head with whom the real control rests? Who is the final decision maker?

This may seem like a funny scenario but trust me, such a scenario actually exists. 'Multi-headed hydra' type organisations or departments do not augur well for the future. Such scenarios breed employee politics and managerial division – as in employees playing one reporting boss against the other. Managers are therefore occupied fighting inter-managerial conflict rather than steering the organisation. Furthermore, in the above scenario, dept. head X can shirk a particular responsibility claiming it to be within the jurisdiction of dept. head Y.

The sad result: *Nobody's baby is equal to organisation's orphan*!!

One of the basic principles of management are 'Unity of Direction' & 'unity of control'. An organism with more than one head is a misfit (and a freak) in our world today and the same applies in management (NGO & corporate alike). You cannot have one group of people reporting to two persons at the same time – a sure shot recipe for a rift within, that will get filled with politics & tension and no single direction for the team. It could be like having one foot on the accelerator & and one on the brake – lots of smoke & little or no forward movement.

Every organisation/department in an NGO must have ONE leader in overall control and all others accountable or reporting in to that leader. The result of a Cerberus leadership situation in the NGO is nobody in real leadership. A classic case where two heads are definitely NOT better than one.

The 'Leadership-phobia' risk

I bet the title of this one has you laughing. "Leadership-phobia", you say? That's like the frightened lion in Wizard of Oz – fairy-tale and funny!

Alas, comical but true. There are those who are appointed as leaders who have a plausible fear of taking decisions. It is not so much the fear of the decision aspect – it's the fear of 'end-result-consequence' that scares such leaders.

The root cause of the 'Leadership-phobia' is the phobia of having to be accountable to the Board of directors/Governing body/ Members for a decision gone wrong and a loss/negative result. It's like the schoolboy frightened of failing the test and being scolded and consequently running away from school to avoid taking the test.

This phobia can paralyse the most well-meaning of leaders, rendering them incompetent at best or obstacles to their own leadership, at worst. Leaders suffering from the 'leadership-phobia' prefer the status-quo as compared to an 'upsetting-the-apple-cart' decision. Irrespective of the hard facts and figures presented to such leaders, their penchant for the pause button is incomparable.

The simplest solution for such a leader, if you are one, is to engage in discussion and the broad-basing of analysis and decision-making. Don't merely broad-base the discussion and then sit on it. Broad-base the decision too but have the courage of your convictions to sign-off on it after a consensus has been achieved.

There is strength in collective wisdom.

Sometimes you can overcome your phobia by finding courage in a committee. The frightened lion didn't find courage on his own but in the company of others and that too on the Yellow Brick Road – not while standing still.

More often than not, fear/phobia is best dealt with by confronting it. As leaders, we must understand and absorb the fact that leadership is more about handling the difficult issues, not so much the easy ones. The easy ones are no-brainers, really!

If leadership was all about easy decisions, they wouldn't need you or me!! In today's hi-tech world, all it would take is a computer with the appropriate configuration & AI (artificial intelligence). You were chosen by your Board of Directors/governing body to be the leader in order to handle the critical/difficult issues, not merely the easy ones. Also know this, that you were chosen because you were considered the best available person to handle the job – including the difficult issues. (Flip back to the 'mantle of control' in this chapter). This was the mandate your governing body/Board gave you – whether written or implied.

To the frightened lions, I would say, step up to the crease, take a deep breath – put willow to the leather and whack that decision ball right out of the park.

'Post-mortem accountability' risk

This risk is more for the apex accountability body of any organisation/NGO (i.e. the Governing body/Board/members). It is the other side of the 'leadership-phobia' coin.

For those of us who find ourselves on such apex accountability bodies, we often take pride in conducting extensive 'post-mortem' analyses on past decisions which have gone south. While nobody disputes the necessity of a post mortem analysis on such decisions, often it is our own blood-lust that we need to satisfy by seeing a person in leadership being subjected to the humiliating 'hanged-drawn-and-quartered' school of torture.

We must refrain from excessively subscribing to the 'off-with-the-head' dialogue of the Red Queen in Lewis Carroll's novel Through the Looking Glass. Such a policy surely gives rise to 'leadership-phobia'.

There are a number of decisions which merit admission of bad decision makers to the school of torture or even the 'off-with-the-head' punishment. However, this is not the acceptable line for each and every decision that goes wrong. Some decisions go bad for reasons completely out of the control of the decision maker/s. It is essential for apex accountability bodies to exercise a judicious sense of balance when concluding which decision went wrong and for what reason/s.

Excessive post-mortem accountability of a leader will result in decision-paralysis and status quo and is best avoided.

The 'Stalinesque' risk

The behavioural opposite of the frightened lion (Leadership phobia) is the fearless lion. Possessing and presenting a visual image & impression of an iron man among minions, this leader exhibits the combined characteristics of many leadership flaws. This leader has a deadly cocktail of 'I-know-it-all' and 'Greater-than-thou' mixed with authoritarianism of Hitler or Stalin. They are the be-all and end-all in their universe and their writ runs large across the NGOs they control. Their wisdom is the only wisdom and their decision is the only decision. Any other voice of wisdom will be sent to the 'gulag' or concentration camp or to be 'executed at dawn'. Stalin's vice-like grip on Russia is legendary and hence the term 'Stalinesque risk'. The Stalinist leader in his so-called managerial wisdom (or blindness) will make far-reaching decisions, based on his own narrow-minded conclusions – decisions that can chain an organisation to the sea-floor amid rising waters. Decisions which will shake the foundations of the NGOs future. I am aware of one particular shocking case where a Stalinist-type leader struck a deal for 10 years, simply because he (alone) was convinced, he was buying 'efficiency' – a deal that still continues to shake that organisation's financials.

There is strength in collective wisdom. Do not allow one leader to become a Hitler or a Stalin.

- - - - -

Leadership risk is possibly the greatest risk of them all – with a weightage of 4 or 5 times the risk associated with any other risk factor. Do you know why?

Recall the illustration of the school bus driver in the previous chapter on Compliance & Legal Risk. The bus driver in the NGO context is its leader or leadership. Leadership is the guiding light or guidance system that, by its actions, determines whether the NGO achieves its objectives or whether its efforts get buried in the dust – well short of the mark.

Realistically, a leader can build up an organisation's human structure or single-handedly tear it down. You may have heard the saying 'a team is only as good as it's leader!' When a team fails, normally it's because the leader has failed. A failed leader in the corporate sector can result in the loss of a few millions but a failed leader in an NGO will result in irreparable, incalculable loss of future for some hundreds of thousands of underprivileged people. The economic & social loss resulting from leadership risk in an NGO just cannot be calculated.

Truth be told, the core philosophy of a leader is actually to make himself 'redundant'. This can only be achieved by leading by example not by diktat. In war, a captain didn't merely send men into battle – he _led_ them into battle. The real leader also, isn't scared of having capable second/s-in-command, which is why the real leader mentors the next line of leadership. In war, it was a captain's duty to prepare & mentor a capable deputy who could pick up the reins and be able to lead the men, should the captain fall to the enemy's bullets – all in a split second.

In reality, the leader who makes himself 'redundant', doesn't actually become redundant but only goes on to become more critical to the team's success. As the leader lifts others up, he gets lifted up himself as the leader of the team.

Lead by wisdom, not by ego!

Chapter XI

Information Technology & Automation Risk

Through the various ages, man has progressed immensely and in leaps and bounds. What was then is not now, and what is now was not then!

If you are a believer in Darwinism, you will agree that civilization has led us down the long winding road from ape to 21st century man. In a lighter vein - we have gone from ape to being 'out of shape'.

We have metamorphosed from the hunter-gatherer way of living to the 'app-order' way of life. Man began this long journey by discovering fire, then inventing tools. Fire led to the forge and some tools became weapons thereby kickstarting the world's unstoppable arms race. Other tools became implements for mining, leading to the discovery of minerals for multiple uses and the systematic plunder of the planet. Discovery led to invention and invention led to discovery in an interminable cycle fuelled by that insatiable engine known as the human brain.

Man journeyed from the Stone Age to the Bronze Age to the Industrial Age to the Technology Age – with a whole lot of other ages in between. Today man seems to have ventured into what I call 'the pseudo-God age', using genetic engineering while attempting to modify the DNA of things, create life from dead things, re-engineer the world's composition and creation.

Nothing, however, has given a boost to the speed of transformation and development than the invention of the computer. The origins of the modern computer (and of course, super-computer) lie with Charles Babbage who is widely acknowledged as the 'father of the computer'. Computing speed did the pole vault with the invention of semi-conductor transistors and 'Integrated Circuits', in the 1940s and 1950s. There has been no looking back since.

Forbes.com website lists the following as some of the best tech innovations of the last three years.

✓ Practical Augmented Reality – dealing with micro-displays and hi-tech personal wearables

✓ Generative Adversarial Networks (GANs) – A new type of neural networking

✓ Real Time Language Translation – Combination of Voice recognition technology and Artificial Intelligence (AI)

✓ Chatbots – The virtual call-centre executive!

✓ Artificial Intelligence in Mobile Apps

✓ Inexpensive, Fast Storage – High-performing, lower cost data storage systems

✓ Deep Learning-Based Predictive Analytics

✓ Serverless Computing

✓ Brain-Computer Interfaces – Dealing with brain scanners translating your thoughts into words/text!

✓ AI and machine learning applications

✓ The Cloud

For someone who is not alien to the world of Information Tech, I nearly fell off my chair at the time of writing this, when I read about 'Brain-Computer Interfaces' and 'Deep Learning-Based Predictive Analytics'.

And you thought the I-Pad 4, the I-Watch, the virtual marketplaces, the mobile apps, etc were the hot tech items of the present time.

Ever since the first computing machine was invented, information technology was set on a breakneck speed of development and along with it the world has been set on the irreversible path of digital transformation.

Why have I spent so many words on introducing this chapter and what does it have to do with Information Technology (IT) risk for the NGO? All of the above are merely to condition your brain to the importance of information technology in today's day and age and the speed with which technology is replaced or rendered redundant, before putting it into perspective for the NGO.

For most of us in our NGOs, IT extends only as far as having desktop computers (or laptops) with printers (standalone or networked) and a Local Area Network (LAN). If deployed properly and utilised well, IT can be a great enabler. It's absence in the NGO can prove to be a great 'disabler' though.

The NGO does not have to be a multinational like Google or Apple Inc., or an Amazon, etc for cutting edge information technology but it must have a judicious use of IT to enable its objectives to be achieved. You don't need the best tech innovations listed above to be IT-savvy.

I am aware of one organisation where IT (and IT based functioning) was not a priority because one leader was a self-confessed 'non-tech-savvy' person and blocked simple IT based improvements for months on end. The same organisation used the age-old system of hand-written letters which would then be hand-delivered, for one of its sub-verticals. To add insult to injury, many of the units of the sub-vertical were based almost a couple of hours (by train) away from the Head Office – causing one employee, from each unit, to travel back and forth to deliver the hand written communications. All of this in the 21st century! This process just may have been more poetic with the use of horseback riders!

It didn't require rocket science to introduce basic level computers and internet facility to upgrade the units from the 'Wild West messenger' service to the 'not so hi-tech email'.

Payroll processing: Some NGOs may still resort to the manual process for payroll, wherein calculation, payment and disbursement of monthly salaries of staff is done manually – using pen and paper. Prima facie this does not seem risky, one might claim. The risks involved are human error in calculation as well as the waste of manhours of one or more staff spending a day or a few days on manual calculation. The logic of such age-old processes defeats me – particularly when there is an abundance of low-cost payroll packages available in the market.

Manual accounting: There are some NGOs which still carry out their day-to-day accounting in the same old fashion as it was done decades ago – with pen and paper, in massive ledgers. Most have since moved on from the muscle-building ledgers to the accounting software on the computer. Give a thought to how cumbersome and time-consuming it is to convert manual accounts to computer-based accounts. In my opinion, converting manual accounts to Excel-based accounts and auditing it, could be classified as a high form of intellectual torture – especially in a large NGO. However, most NGOs worth their salt would have taken the step of computerised accounting some years ago. For those yet to follow suit, the time for this was *yesterday*!

Half-baked software: Have you ever tried eating a half-baked cake?

In an off-shoot to manual accounting, the sad truth for a good number of NGOs lies in the fact that their accounting is computerised – but with 'half-baked' software. I am aware of at least two such entities (out of a number of them), both of which use computerised accounting systems. Unfortunately, these accounting systems don't go to the 'hilt'. One software prepares the vouchers and provides some reports but stops after the Receipts & Payments account. Neither does it match cash payments against software issued cash vouchers. There is no Income & Expenditure Account, no Trial Balance, no Balance Sheet either – all of these are manually prepared.

Another one goes a step further and incorporates billing but billing module and payments against billing just doesn't feed automatically into the accounting software. Different software modules are operating in isolation! The extracts from billing needs to be manually entered in the computerised accounts on periodical basis and then the Trial Balance gets generated. This software does not go as far as a Receipts & Payments account, let alone an Income & Expenditure Account or Balance Sheet.

"So what?", you may say. It would take a little more effort from the accounts staff, you say, to finalize the accounts. Where's the risk in that?

Take the case of the second illustration. Billing and payment data need to be manually entered into the accounting software.

Risk 1: An accountant forgets to enter the figures for one day and nobody is aware of it.

Risk 2: Cashier and accountant are working in collusion to game the system. Billing Cashier shows the day's collections of INR 500,000 in cash in the billing module and the accountant shows the collections as INR 450,000 in the accounting module. Each pockets a cool INR 25000 in a day assuming they split the difference down the middle.

Risk 3: Revenue figures can be inflated to paint a rosy picture of the organisation, whereas the real finances may be a 'black-hole', thereby misleading all and sundry including bankers and the organisation's apex body. Until it is too late that is.

Risk 4: The outstanding dues of debtors may be reduced in exchange of financial favours.

Risk 5: Fraudulent creditors may be created in the software – vendors who may be owed money without actually supplying anything!

Now, let's look at the first Illustration. It seems more robust compared to the second. In reality, not so.

Risk 1: What gets accounted for is only that which is input in the software. Something may be missed out – accidentally or deliberately. A bill could be misplaced or destroyed, hence never entered, never paid, never due.

Risk 2: Cash received by the cashier may not be reported at all to the accountant for entering in the computer software. The misappropriation will NEVER be discovered.

Risk 3: Against a software generated combined-cash-voucher of INR 50,000 for amounts payable to multiple parties, the cashier may pay only INR 45,000, thereby pocketing the difference.

Half-baked software usually results from someone's total ignorance of software or a shortage of funds or else from someone's unscrupulous nature. The first two reasons don't need explanation, the third does. It is possible for an unscrupulous leader to deliberately block completion of a customised accounting software, so as to exploit the gaps for personal financial gain.

Whatever the reason for a half-baked software, where yawning gaps exist due to it, these will be exploited by the unscrupulous.

ERP software: Now this one is not for all NGOs to adopt and hence isn't a risk for the greater majority of NGO entities. ERP stands for 'Enterprisewide-Resource-Planning' or in simple terms, the application of IT in linking all facets/segments of the organisation, so that resources are not wasted but optimal use of resources takes place. This results in greater efficiency and substantial cost savings in the medium to long run. However, ERP software tends to cost a 'bomb', to implement and maintain. ERP is best used by NGO-run-hospitals and NGOs with a strong manufacturing setup. Typically, a hospital would need to link its in-patient admission, diagnosis, clinical tests, pharmacy issuances, all applicable (rendered) services with its billing and payments setup. This would then feed into the requirement for medicines, medical supplies, surgical (and non-surgical) equipment, oxygen, linen, etc, complete with inventory planning and re-order levels and purchase order issuance.

Web-presence: The internet or the world-wide-web began dominating our computer screens since the 1980s and has since taken pride of place on the mobile too. Most of us cannot do without turning on 'mobile data' and surfing the net or checking email/WhatsApp, etc. Despite mobile internet usage running away with itself, there are many NGOs which are yet to come up with their own presence on the web. Having a website for your NGO is not just necessary, it is downright critical. Make no mistake, your website does not tell the world that your NGO has arrived – it merely says "Hey, we are there too". The basic risk of a zero web-presence is that potential donors can't find you.

The greater risk, though, lies in having a 'static website' – a website which exists with your NGO's basic information (or all of it) put up on a one-time basis, and updates to the website made on half-yearly or annually. Donors today would like to check your website at least once a month or once a fortnight for updates on how things are going. Is their donation being wisely used and how?

Your website can also be used to market your NGO through low cost web-advertisement – it's an excellent mass-market tool.

No Tech person on board: This one isn't really an IT risk, in the core sense of the term but it's a vital pillar, the absence of which contributes substantially to IT risk. It is always advisable to have a qualified person in charge of an Information Technology department in the organisation or else to assign the role to someone with a reasonably strong IT knowledge or else appoint a part-time consultant for the job. The person should be tasked with keeping upto-date with trends in IT and ascertaining whether any new development in the field could render the organisation's technology redundant or archaic and recommend suitable upgrades from time to time. Not having such a person will directly result in an organisation getting cheated on price, quality and configuration of IT items purchased. You could be sold an obsolete laptop for an attractive price, with a configuration that went out of date 6 months ago. You would probably end up buying it, because the 'attractive' price would sway you. Alternately, I know of a case where a software developer was paid 75% of the contract price for developing a customised payroll software, even before the software could be tested. When a person with IT knowledge was brought into the picture, it came to light that the 75% had been paid, whereas even the basic building block (i.e. the database structure) for the software had not been created by the developer. Money had been paid on the software developer's certifications with nobody from the organisation to cross check the ground reality. This is just one illustration of many which I can place before you.

Last mile delivery mechanism: As an ex-banker from Private sector banks, I am well-versed with the manner in which Indian private sector banks have used Information Technology to radically transform the way we bank and the way these banks do business. One such bank (which I am personally proud to have worked in) is HDFC Bank, which uses a very robust IT backbone for customers as well as for internal purposes. As an employee, we had the advantage of loads of information at our fingertips through something called the 'information portal', which gave you access to operational circulars, product features, leave request system, special communications, your own pay-slips, stationery indents, etc. The greater majority of these things would otherwise have been processed through the manual (paper-based) system with tons of paper flowing back and forth for each and everything. By leveraging IT, the bank managed to empower its employees substantially and cut down on inefficient methods drastically, as well as save time and money.

As an NGO, you need to take a look at what your last mile delivery is and how this is currently being achieved. NGOs which have children's education sponsorship programmes or village development programmes need to actively reconsider how they deliver reports to their donors. If it has been happening in the age-old paper-based system, it's high time to re-engineer the last mile delivery mechanism. This would need to tie-in with a dynamic website to provide your donor (anywhere in the world) access to the happenings in your project/s on a day-to-day/week-to-week basis. A robust last mile delivery mechanism reporting real-time good results promotes a feel-good factor with donors and *feel-good often translates into donate-more*!

Automation Risk: Going back to the banking example again, a couple of decades ago banking practices for customers entailed personally going to the bank, filling in a deposit/withdrawal slip, taking a number token, standing in the bank waiting for the number to be called, then go to teller counter for cash deposit or withdrawal. If you were withdrawing cash, the teller would look at you very suspiciously and check three times before paying you your own money – after all wasn't the bank doing you a favour by paying you? In the mid-1990s, along came the Private sector banks which literally put the customer on a pedestal. To make your life convenient, they introduced ATMs so you could withdraw cash far from the bank branch. Next came Phone banking, Internet banking and mobile banking – bank away from the bank!

Now, when you need help on a banking matter, you can chat online with the bank's virtual assistant (by whatever name) on the bank's website. There is no physical person chatting with you – it's a computer program, using AI, and it's called a 'chatbot'. This is called automation.

Another prime example of automation, is the Uber app – to hire a taxi cab to take you to office or anywhere else. Before, to hail a cab one stood on the street and waved frantically to get a passing cabbie's attention and more often than not had to argue with the insolent/ arrogant driver, who would quote exorbitant prices. To add insult to injury, the cab in question would be a non-AC one. The old process = Hail a cab + argue with cabbie + get fleeced + sweat it out, etc.

Enter automation/disruptive technology a.k.a. the Uber app. Process = turn on GPS and mobile data on your mobile phone + open Uber app + enter destination + accept fare + wait for cab to arrive + check cab and driver details + travel to destination in AC comfort + pay online + rate the driver. Though the price is higher than a non-AC cab (without being fleeced), it's a great way to travel.

Why in a book for NGOs am I talking about all this? Automation has a disruptive face to it. It turns the old way of doing things on its head. In the above illustration, old banks (which were now in competition with the new private banks) had to radically change their ways of doing business since they began to lose customers by the thousands. In the Uber app example, the result is many yellow taxi cabs have gone out of business.

As an NGO, you may have been doing your business/social service in a particular manner for decades. Along comes another NGO with the same activity and it embraces IT, automating its processes in a manner which provides for greater ground level control, efficiency, quicker data capture & faster result delivery to stakeholders. They are the 'new-private-sector-bank' while you are the 'old-bank'.

Your data will take many weeks/months to reach your donors. Their data/updates will take hours/few days to reach their patrons. The best publicity is word-of-mouth publicity and you will steadily lose your 'business' to them. Your donors will shift base to them because they are more efficient and quicker to the finishing line. Your experience/vintage in the business counts for nothing when automation renders you obsolete. Thanks to automation you just became a fossil and you can now add the word 'Jurassic' to your entity name. Automation can kill your NGO. Disruptive Technology (a.k.a. automation) is here to stay – it's the way of the future, embrace it.

Information Technology – for the NGO it's presence can be a great enabler.
Its absence will be your great 'disabler'.

Chapter XII

Risks from Governmental Action, Corporate Action & Judicial Consequence

Anyone who is a fan of the cooking competition/TV show – MasterChef Australia – would be all too familiar with the words "Boom, boom, shake the room!". Typically used when the judges want the contestants to come up with something extraordinary and figuratively 'shake the room' with the quality of food they put up.

Well, that's about as far as the culinary introduction would go for this chapter – which is not about food but really about *the shaking of the room*. Seriously enough, have you actually been through a 'shake the room' experience? Experienced an earthquake – when everything shook around you? I don't know about you, but I have – in a ninth-floor office cabin, quite high above the ground – and it plays games with your sense of balance, sort of destabilizing. Experiencing a moderately severe earthquake (let alone a severe one & so high up) can give anyone the shivers or promptly bring the name of your god/creator to mind.

In a NGO scenario, statutory & legal compliance is crazy enough, but what happens when the very ground below you – the one on which you function – actually shakes (figuratively that is)? Your compliance record may be good or near perfect but along comes some new regulation that leaves you suspended in mid-air, with that sickening feeling of nothing below except empty space? And then gravity takes over. Recall something like that? For NGOs running schools, you may be familiar with the introduction of the RTE (Right of Children to Free & Compulsory Education) Act of 2009. For every non-minority, *non-profit* NGO with schools, this piece of legislation threw a massive spanner into their future income-expenditure projections. 25% seats to be reserved to provide for education for poor children without access to education – free of charge, as well as provide for playground, midday meals, separate toilets, etc. Say what?

Risks from such unforeseen developments as these can actually blow our functional, time-tested models and immediate operations to smithereens, leaving us picking up the pieces. Such risks can arise from governmental action or corporate action/legislation or even judicial action.

This chapter does not endeavour to analyse the rationale of any legislation or governmental action nor does it attempt to look into the merits or de-merits of the same. It merely seeks to focus on the impact/risks that arise to NGOs in their functioning, from such actions (whether governmental, corporate or even judicial).

Governmental Action

Let's begin by taking a look at a governmental action such as the currency demonetisation launched in our country in November 2016. Now that was a massive exercise that saw people queuing up at banks to deposit old (demonetised) currency and withdraw new currency. Demonetisation…and the NGO – relevance? How does that add up? As an NGO, let's say you were:

a. paying your monthly staff salaries in cash for many years, not even by cheque. OR

b. Paying small amounts as monthly benevolence/food support allowances by cash OR

c. Paying electricity bills in cash OR

d. Receiving school fees mostly in cash OR

e. Reimbursing conveyance and incidental expenses to poor patients for hospital visits OR

f. Any other such cash-based payment or receipt.

I do believe most of these things were rather common occurrence till then. All these practices were dealt a crippling blow by demonetisation – with the sudden clampdown on cash withdrawal amounts per week and the documentation needed for deposit of 'old' or demonetised currency.

One of the impacts of demonetisation which is still fresh in my mind, is the dilemma we faced with payment of a few people's salaries. What was till then an age-old and time-tested practice was now a problem of epic proportions. A small team, led by this author, swung into action by first putting the problem aside and then focussing on a workable solution. In less than 10 days, this solution was brought to fulfilment and implemented in time for disbursement of the November 2016 payroll – fully resolving the cash problem. The solution wasn't just a quick fix but a permanent solution for all time.

Schools which had for ages received fees in cash & cheque (predominantly cash) found themselves staring down a double-barrelled gun being unable to receive fees in cash and also unable to take action against fee defaulters, since cash was in scarce supply for the months in question. These schools were forced to look at alternative solutions such as payment by debit cards & credit cards (POS machines) and receipt of fees by NEFT or even through setup of payment gateways. Hospitals which received patients' payments primarily in cash had to switch to payment by plastic (POS machines) and given the massive spurt in demand, banks were just not geared to meet the demand for these machines quickly enough.

A couple of years later another piece of major governmental legislation called the 'Goods & Service Tax (GST)' came into being. The GST Act provided for relief for NGOs which were registered under Section 12AA of the Income Tax Act, 1961 AND which were doing *charitable activities*. The common perception (or mis-perception) was that all NGOs registered under this section 12AA were given a 'blanket-exemption' from GST and hence did not need to register under the GST Act, and that GST was not their headache. Moreover, the vast majority of NGOs had never come under the Service Tax umbrella, which muddied the 'perception waters' some more. Some very old entities which were registered under Section 12A of the Income Tax Act 1961, may not have registered under Section 12AA (which was a section introduced later) – which now presented a possible legal problem.

Whatever the case may have been for any NGO, GST was one earth-shaking piece of legislation which changed forever the way the NGOs worked. The simplicity of the exempt or not exempt (i.e. a plain 'yes or no' answer or an 'it's black or white') was no longer satisfactory. With GST rules, your entity could be exempt as well as non-exempt. Confusing? If you were registered under section 12AA and conducting charitable activities as defined by the GST Act, then those activities would be exempt from GST. However, any activity not listed as a charitable activity in that list meant you were liable to charge GST, even if you were registered under section 12AA. For example, a section 12AA registered religious trust/society obtaining advertisement for a social event not relating to the advancement of religion, such advertisement would be liable to GST being chargeable. The same would be applicable to a section 12AA registered hospital/society charging rent from a party for lease of a portion of its premises for say ATM/bank/canteen, etc. Every NGO needed to take a relook at its functioning and the applicability of GST to all aspects of it, as well as the necessary infrastructure (including software systems) and man-power to ensure compliance.

A decade ago, the government passed the revised FCRA Act 2010, which specified a validity date for all existing FCRA registrations. These certificates/registrations which previously did not require renewal, now require renewal every 5 years. As on date of writing, there were more than 6400 such entities whose FCRA certificate have become invalid/registration has been deemed to have ceased. (source: fcraonline.nic.in). If each of these entities served just 10 (ten) underprivileged people each, 64000 people have been impacted adversely or not been positively impacted with life change. This is not the fault of the government but a direct result of the risk that possibly has resulted from a lack of prompt response to governmental action or the lack of knowledge for timely and adequate response.

The same website shows a whopping 20600+ entities which, since 2011, have had their FCRA licences cancelled – i.e. in 8 years, for violations or cancelled on request. The vast majority of these 20600+ entities are for violations of the FCRA Act. A stunning 1800+ entities have had their registration cancelled in 2019 alone.

Yet again, a few years ago, the government issued rules for submission of FCRA annual returns (and quarterly returns) to be made online only. NGOs with FCRA registration which, for years, were well-versed in the procedure of submission of annual returns in hard-copy continued to skirt the new procedures, only to their detriment. As on date of writing, there were more than 800 such entities which had not submitted their Annual Returns for 2017–18 to the Ministry of Home Affairs (source: fcraonline.nic.in). Some of these entities would possibly be non-functional but the balance would be lacking the expertise to comply with the online mode.

The FCRA Act 2010 was another 'earth-shaking' piece of legislation for the NGO sector, as it tightened/revamped procedures, reporting and penalties.

Corporate Action

With the action on the local funding front shifting to CSR or Corporate Social Responsibility, there are risks which can arise from Corporate Action too. The government notified Section 135 of the Companies Act 2013, with the Companies (Corporate Social Responsibility Policy) Rules effective from 1 April 2014, whereby companies under the Act with certain minimum turnover or net profit would have to spend minimum 2% (of the average profit of last 3 years) on the various activities listed by the rules. This was mandatory under the Act & the Rules.

This was an excellent, very positive development for the NGO sector but not without its risks. How so, one may ask, since it's a very good source of funds for a sector that is essentially starved for funds.

Suppose your NGO has obtained a grant/donation of INR 1 crore (10 million) from XYZ Ltd., for the financial year. Your programme/project has budgeted for this level of expenditure per year for the next three years with the assumption that this is a given. The economy hits a severe rut and XYZ Ltd., is hit by a huge loss in the next financial year, resulting in the 3-year average profit falling big time and your CSR funding in the next year taking a severe hit.

Alternately, what if the corporate funding your education/drinking water/ healthcare/other project, through CSR, suddenly decides they have put CSR funds into x project for the last 3 years continuously and therefore should shift focus to another segment on the permissible CSR activities list, such as clean drinking water. What happens to your project? Where you had seemingly 'assured' project funding, you now have a great big hole in your project's wallet. The worst part of all this is you can't do a thing about it, since you are merely a beneficiary and cannot decide the corporate's CSR funding avenues.

Or what if the corporate action risk is not about CSR but the result of corporate research and development. What if some company comes out with a product that renders your NGO model totally redundant?

Let's say your entity is a hospital specializing in cardiac treatment such as surgery for 'heart-block' or clogged arteries and some company comes out with a cheap/subsidized wonder drug to cure this in 3 months, without a need for surgery. Your business model goes straight down the toilet. No more surgeries, very little revenue from the segment, same staff cost and a big fat loss staring you in the face. Again, what if you are into safe drinking water through providing a bulky, heavy non-electricity powered water-filter to poor people and some company comes along with a solar-powered portable water filter. Business model down the toilet again.

Judicial Action

This one seems quite obvious. From time to time, our apex Court (The Supreme Court of India) takes a view on certain critical aspects in the country and passes landmark judgements which affect the way we function.

One such recent, landmark judgement was the Supreme Court's observation on what constitutes basic wages as far as calculation of Provident Fund is concerned (dealt with in the Chapter titled 'Compliance & Legal Risk'). This impacted the age-old method of calculation of PF and resulted in additional financial outgo for NGOs, on PF.

In October 2018, the Supreme Court banned the use of 15-year old petrol vehicles & 10-year old diesel vehicles from plying in New Delhi-NCR region. According to news reports, in November 2019 the Bihar government has followed suit and banned 15-year old vehicles across the state including government vehicles. If your NGO in Bihar uses a vehicle which is more than 15 years old, you have suffered from judicial action risk.

Similarly, what about the Supreme Court's observations on the RTE Act 2009 applicability to minority run schools? The apex court's ruling made some of the Act's provisions applicable to such institutions (dealt with in the section 'RTE Act as applicable to Minority institutions' in the chapter titled 'Compliance & Legal Risk') even though they were exempted under Article 30 of the Constitution of India.

- - - - -

So, what does one effectively do, when unforeseen 'earth-shaking' actions occur, which alter the very nature of the NGO playing field? How do you hedge the risk from the 'unforeseen'?

The fact of the matter is that you can't avoid all risks, particularly the unforeseen ones. If you could, then you might be God or the one-eyed man in the land of the blind! Each and every one of these instances or examples which have been cited above, all have one word to describe them – disruption! Indeed, much like the example of the Uber app which disrupted the old ways of the taxi cab business, each unforeseen action whether governmental or corporate or judicial represents 'disruption' to the existing way/s in which we do business.

However, we still need to do something about the risk from these events.

As far as governmental action and judicial action go, there can be no prescribed method to minimise the risk or no prescribed risk-avoidance measure. The best that can be done is 'risk minimisation by response'. If you find yourself on the wrong side of a sudden governmental action, the way in which you respond/react will determine the quantum of risk you bear. It is essential to first fully understand what the governmental/judicial action is about and how it will impact you. If necessary, obtain an expert's opinion to determine the impact on your NGO and then consider possible solutions and decide on the best one. Generally, with important legislation it is never a surprise affair and such legislation takes weeks and months to wind its way through parliamentary procedures before becoming law. During this time, it attracts press coverage through print and TV media. Therefore, keep up to date on current affairs by reading one national newspaper & one widely read current affairs magazine a month. If you find anything that may impact your entity's functioning, consult an expert beforehand. This should enable you to stay 'ahead of the curve', so to speak.

As far as CSR funding is concerned, some degree of risk mitigation is possible by building in clauses into the MOU between your NGO and the corporate, which require a minimum notice period before stoppage of funding and/or a certain minimum commitment in terms of amounts and timelines. These will enable the NGO to search for alternative avenues of funding to bridge any possible funds mismatch, well in advance.

The basic remedy for all of these unforeseen actions, however, is to be fleet-footed in your mind – react quickly (though not knee-jerk reaction). Don't run to court – resolve the problem at hand as far as possible, then litigate. Litigation must not be the first option, it's the last – since litigation proceedings take far too long.

To end on a lighter note, the solution to the unforeseen risk lies in an old nursery rhyme (though slightly modified here).

"Jack-be-nimble-Jack-be-quick, Jack jump over the unforeseen-(risk)-stick"

Chapter XIII

Investment Risk

For many NGOs, money is that commodity/resource which is always in short supply. However, that is not to say that 365 days of the year you are 'funds negative'. There are always times in the year when one donor will send you a bulk amount of money for a longer-term purpose or a utilisation period which stretches across a few months. Such funds are 'designated funds' and can't be used for general expenses and hence these funds are surplus till required as per the project's expenditure timeline. What we do with that surplus till the time of expenditure determines whether or not we are subjecting our organisations to investment risk.

To many NGO people, investment merely entails booking a Fixed deposit for x days in some bank. Is that the only avenue of investment available to NGOs? If that be the case, I know a whole barnyard of bankers who would be chasing NGOs like foxes chase rabbits!

For one specific source of funds, there is no alternative available to NGOs except to book Fixed Deposits – that of FCRA funds, or funds received from overseas donors. These funds are regulated by the FCRA act and investment for purposes which can be viewed as 'speculative' are banned by law. Therefore, investment of surplus FCRA funds in equities, mutual funds (whether debt or equity), short or medium-term real estate, ULIPs, etc are strict no-nos – unless you wish to run the gauntlet and lose your FCRA registration.

So, what exactly constitutes investment risk for the NGO? Let's take a look.

Loss of investment income from idle funds: Believe it or not, but there are some NGOs which leave massive idle funds lying around in their Savings & Current accounts. Well, what's wrong with that you may say? Go back to Chapter 3: Financial Risk, to the part on OCHR. Assume for a moment that your NGO has a regular balance of INR 5 million (Rs. 50 lakhs) in your Bank account, which is a savings account paying 4% p.a. interest. On a rough calculation, you would earn Rs. 200,000 as interest in the account. Assume that INR 4 million (Rs. 40 lakhs) is surplus funds for deployment after 6 months, this amount can be placed in Fixed Deposits at say 6%, you would earn a total interest of Rs. 120,000 on the Rs. 40 lakhs (for 6 months) instead of just Rs. 80,000 for six months @ 4% p.a. The additional forty thousand rupees earned can be deployed for various other purposes.

The loss of income is massive if you have a Current Account, which pays you zero interest on your account balances, instead of a Savings Bank Account. This principle applies to both surplus FCRA funds and non-FCRA funds. Check with your banker whether your NGO bank account is a Current Account or a Savings Bank account.

I am aware of no less than 3 such organisations which leave large amounts of surplus funds in their Savings/Current accounts. We all know the saying 'a penny saved is a penny earned'. How about coining a new one here – a penny earned is a penny well saved!

Incorrect investment term horizon: One very common mistake made by NGOs is the term horizon for an investment, irrespective of the nature of investment. In other words, you have surplus funds which you know will be required for utilisation in a project six months later. The resultant fixed deposit which gets booked with the bank is for one year. This is a classic ALM story or Asset-Liability-Management – a mismatch in this case. You have a projected liability (or in this case expenditure) in 6 months but the Asset (in this case the FD) has not been booked for 6 months – to mature at the time of the funds outflow requirement, but six months later.

So, what, you might say – just break the Fixed Deposit after six months. Easier said than done.

There are two aspects here which need consideration. The first is the concept of applicable interest rate. When you book a Fixed Deposit for one year, let's say you receive an interest rate of 6% p.a. on that deposit. On the date of booking the Fixed Deposit, let's say the interest rate for a 6-month FD was 5% p.a. When the 1-year Fixed deposit is broken or liquidated prematurely after 6 months, you will not get interest paid to you at the interest rate at which the FD was booked (i.e. 6% p.a.) for half the year. Instead, you will get interest paid at the 'applicable rate' for six months – i.e. @ 5% p.a., for 6 months.

The second aspect you need to be aware of is penalty interest on an FD prematurely broken. Some banks levy a penalty interest ranging from 0.25% to 1%. Therefore, when you break the one-year FD after six months, if the bank has a penalty interest clause of 1%, you will end up receiving the applicable rate less the penalty interest. In the above example, you would get 5% p.a. less 1% p.a. penalty, for six months (i.e. net 2% interest only on the FD or 2.5% applicable rate for 6 months less 0.5% penalty for 6 months).

Why do banks charge a FD premature closure penalty? The concept of ALM mentioned above is banking terminology. When you place a FD with a bank for 1 year, it becomes the bank's liability (since they owe you that amount) which is projected to be repayable after 1 year. Ideally, the bank looks for assets to invest/loans to make which are of a 1-year time frame, so that these will mature in time to make the repayment to you. Since you have withdrawn the FD in 6 months (instead of 1 year), the bank's ALM calculations have been upset and the bank will need to either a) borrow from elsewhere to repay you or b) sell the asset earlier than planned, maybe at a loss. Therefore, for upsetting the bank's ALM calculation setup, the depositor (you) have to bear a penalty.

Both applicable rate & penalty interest rate represent a time horizon investment risk. It is best to plan/budget carefully before choosing an investment time frame for surplus funds, to avoid this kind of risk.

Real Rate of Interest

What's a real rate of interest? Isn't the rate of interest you get on an investment, the real rate of interest?

There is a financial concept called the 'time value of money'. This concept basically says the amount of money you receive one year later will actually not have the same value as it has today. This is primarily due to the negative impact of inflation over time. A basket of goods which you can buy today for Rs. 1000 will end up costing more than Rs. 1000 one year from now. Inflation has therefore reduced the value of the money over a period of time.

Therefore, when you invest the surplus funds of your NGO, ensure to ascertain the rate of interest on the investment and also the prevailing rate of inflation in the economy. For example, if the interest rate on your bank Fixed Deposit is 7.0% per annum and the inflation rate in the economy is 3.5%, then your real rate of interest will be 3.5% (i.e. 7% minus 3.5%).

It is important to know this particularly for future period budgeting. If for the next financial period, you are not factoring in the increased/inflation adjusted costs of items, then you need to consider the real amount of interest you will get (after inflation) on your investments. This will ensure parity in the time value of expenses as of today, with the time value of your interest on investments also as of today.

Knowledge on Interest Rate Trends

In-depth knowledge and understanding of interest rate movements and forecasting of its trends is the subject matter for economists and financial experts. However, this author strongly advises that every NGO leader be familiar with developments in the economy, without being an expert. The reason for this is your return on investments can depend on this knowledge. For example, if the economy is doing well and there is a strong demand for loans/funding by companies, the supply of money will be lower than the demand for money and banks will go all out to raise more money for them to lend and will raise fixed deposit rates. If rates are likely to go up within a couple of months, place your surplus funds for only that period of time and reinvest it once the rates move up. This will provide higher returns for your NGOs surplus funds. If you placed your funds for a longer term before the rates moved up, you might face penalty interest as well as applicable rate for your surplus funds. It will nullify any gains from a higher interest rate.

If the economy is slowing down, the Reserve Bank of India may be under pressure to reduce interest rates, so that borrowing becomes cheaper for companies and they are induced to borrow and increase production, thereby boosting the economy. With such a scenario, it would be advisable to place surplus funds at the highest prevailing rate of interest, for a longer-term period subject to your NGOs ALM matching. This way, you will not be caught on the wrong side of the interest rate movement.

You can also keep track of possible interest rate trends through your local bank manager where your NGO account is maintained.

Non-Specified Investments Risk

NGOs have to be especially carefully where they invest. Section 11 of the Income Tax Act 1961, allows for exemption from tax for 'income derived from property held under trust for charitable or religious purposes...... (in India)'. When calculating the total income of the trust/NGO, such income is to be excluded from the calculation. However, there is a rider/condition – which is found in section 11(1)(a) of the Income Tax Act 1961 – 85% of the total income must be utilised for charitable or religious purposes within the country, within the year of receipt. Only 15% of the total income therefore is permitted to be carried forward for utilisation in the next year/subsequent years (maximum 5 years). Funds carried forward (and even surplus funds received during a year) can only be invested in investment avenues specified by the Income Tax Act 1961, in section 11(5).

Should the investment avenue/s differ from the ones laid down by the Act in section 11(5), the incomes from the 'non-specified' investments will be added on in calculation of total income of the trust/NGO and *be taxed*. The entity could even earn the wrath of the tax-man.

Broadly, under section 11(5) of the Income Tax Act, the specified or permitted investment avenues are as follows (abridged & in brief).

(i) investment in savings certificates (section 2 (c) Government Savings Certificates Act, 1959) and any other securities or certificates issued by the Central Government under the Small Savings Schemes of that Government;

(ii) deposits in any Post Office Savings Bank account;

(iii) deposit in any account with a scheduled bank or a co-operative society engaged in carrying on the business of banking;

(iv) investment in units of the Unit Trust of India established under the Unit Trust of India Act, 1963 (52 of 1963);

(v) investment in any security for money created and issued by the Central Government or a State Government;

(vi) investment in debentures issued by, or on behalf of, any company or corporation both the principle whereof and the interest whereon are fully and unconditionally guaranteed by the Central Government or by a State Government;

(vii) investment or deposit in any public sector company;

(viii) deposits with or investment in any bonds issued by a financial corporation which is engaged in providing long-term finance for industrial development in India (and approved by the Central Government);

(ix) deposits with or investment in any bonds issued by a public company formed and registered in India with the main object of carrying on the business of providing long- term finance for construction or purchase of houses in India for residential purposes (and approved by the Central Government);

(x) investment in immovable property.

(xi) deposits with the Industrial Development Bank of India established under the Industrial Development Bank of India Act, 1964

(xii) any other form or mode of investment or deposit as may be prescribed.]

Section 11(5) makes it clear what's allowed as investment, given that you wish to avail of the exemption on the income from such investments.

Speculative Investments

If your NGO has a FCRA account, you must be aware that in the FCRA Act, section 8(1a) bars any foreign contribution or income arising out of it to be used for speculative purposes and Rules of April 2011 – Rule 4 – specifically defines speculative activities, wherein first and foremost, Rule 4a says a speculative activity is "any activity or investment that has an element of risk of appreciation or depreciation of the original investment, linked to market forces, including investments in mutual funds or in shares;"

In plain and simple English, this means that any activity or investment where there is a risk of the original investment/amount going up or down, which is linked to market forces, is a speculative investment.

The Cambridge English Dictionary provides the finance meaning of speculation as follows.

"the act of buying something hoping that its value will increase and then selling at this higher price in order to make a profit:"

(source: https://dictionary.cambridge.org/dictionary/english/speculation)

In other words, considering the pure definition of the root verb 'speculation' (from which the word 'speculative' is derived) and Rule 4a, if you have bought something or made an investment or undertaken an activity, linked to market forces, wherein the expectation is that the price will increase and you will make a profit, then you are engaging in a speculative activity.

On account of the market forces, the value of the investment may go up (resulting in a profit) or may come down (resulting in a loss). Either of the two scenarios are non-desirable, since NGOs are not-for-profit entities – which is the basic rationale for tax exemptions to charitable and religious entities. Furthermore, this is under the FCRA Act and rules, and if an NGO entity brings in foreign funds and uses it for a speculative activity, foreign funded speculative activities are neither charitable nor religious and such activities are liable to regulation under other stringent non-FCRA laws.

It is therefore crucial for every NGO manager/leader to carefully examine the nature of a potential investment avenue before parking any surplus funds in it.

Rule 4(2) of the same FCRA Rules allows for debt-based investments as not speculative. The rule says "A debt-based secure investment shall not be treated as speculative investment".

While this rule is a relief, there is one essential word which must be given high cognizance to – the word 'secure'. There are debt-based investments and debt-based investments and then there are *junk-bonds*! The last one is a highly risky & speculative investment. How does one distinguish between a secure debt-based investment, and insecure debt-based investment and a junk bond? Debt based securities and bonds are required to obtain something called a credit rating from a rating agency, before it can open for subscription. Also, the credit rating has to be printed on the application form for subscription to the securities/bonds. A very high/highest credit rating is most desirable while a low one is an absolute no-go. Look at the ratings assigned by ratings agencies to the investments of a bond before putting your NGO's money in (you can Google the rating to ascertain more detailed information).

In a world where there are so many investment options available and so many investment agents/financial planners to 'convince' you of how terrific their investment option is, one can make a fatal mistake of investing in a forbidden instrument – at great risk to the organisation. Here's a relatively simple table to help you understand where to (and where not to) put your entity's money.

Investment avenue	Nature of investment	Permitted/not permitted	Risk factor/ rationale/points to consider
Equity shares (even blue chip or top-notch companies)	Equity	Not permitted Speculative Not in the permitted list under Section 11(5)	100% linked to share markets and prone to risk.
Mutual fund – Growth (100%)	Equity	Not permitted Speculative Not in the permitted list under Section 11(5)	100% an equity fund, linked to share markets and prone to risk.
Mutual fund – Balanced (50%)	50% equity 50% debt securities	Not permitted Speculative Not in the permitted list under Section 11(5)	50% is in equity, linked to share markets and prone to risk.
Mutual fund – Balanced (10%)	10% equity 90% debt securities	Not permitted Speculative Not in the permitted list under Section 11(5)	10% is in equity, linked to share markets and prone to risk.
Mutual fund – debt	100% debt securities AAA rating	Not Permitted Not in the permitted list under Section 11(5)	*Debt based, secure investment* because of very high rating but income will not be exempt from tax
Mutual fund – fund of funds	Invests in multiple mutual fund schemes	Not permitted Speculative Not in the permitted list under Section 11(5)	Could be entirely debt based or equity based or a mix of both.

Continued...

Index fund	A mutual fund which invests money is based on the composition of an index (e.g. Nifty, Sensex, etc)	Not permitted Speculative Not in the permitted list under Section 11(5)	Could be entirely debt based or equity based or a mix of both.
National Savings Certificates/ National Savings Scheme	Issued by Central Govt	Permitted under Section 11(5) Not Speculative	Investment time period is generally five years – NGO's 15% income, if carried forward, must be utilised within 5 years or becomes taxable.
Post Office Savings Bank account deposit	Govt owned entity	Permitted under Section 11(5) Not Speculative	
Fixed deposit in a scheduled bank or a co- operative society (carrying on the business of banking)	Banks named in the Reserve Bank of India's Second Schedule	Permitted under Section 11(5) Not Speculative	Generally, the most favoured option for NGOs, though interest rates tend to be low. Very easy to do ALM matching Recommended to avoid cooperative banks/societies

Investment in any security created & issued by Central/State Government	Central & State Govt.'s issue long/medium term bonds for subscription	Permitted under Section 11(5) Not Speculative	Such bonds are generally long terms & ALM matching will be a problem. Also, the NGO's 15% income, if carried forward, must be utilised within 5 years or becomes taxable.
Investment in debentures of any company/ corporation	Pre-condition is Principal & interest must be fully and unconditionally guaranteed by the Central/State Govt.	Permitted under Section 11(5) Not Speculative	ALM matching is essential. Also, the interest rate may be low as it carries a Govt. guarantee.
Investment or deposit in any public sector company	Public sector companies are essentially govt. owned	Permitted under Section 11(5) Not Speculative	ALM matching is essential.
Deposits with/ investment in bonds issued by a financial corporation	This corporation must provide long- term finance for industrial development in India & be approved by the Central Govt.	Permitted under Section 11(5) Not Speculative	Such bonds are generally long term & ALM matching will be a problem. Also, the NGO's 15% income, if carried forward, must be utilised within 5 years or becomes taxable.

Continued…

Deposits with/ investment in bonds issued by an Indian public company	This company must provide long- term finance for construction or purchase of houses in India for residential purposes & be approved by the Central Govt.	Permitted under Section 11(5) Not Speculative	Such bonds are generally long terms & ALM matching will be a problem. Also, the NGO's 15% income, if carried forward, must be utilised within 5 years or becomes taxable.
Investment in immovable property	Not including plant & machinery	Permitted under Section 11(5) Not Speculative	Precaution: Avoid investing in immovable property merely for the sake of investment (specially FCRA funds), as it may be considered speculative as immoveable property prices can fluctuate greatly, leading to loss. Investment in immovable property should preferably be in line with the objectives of the NGO.
Deposits with the Industrial Development Bank of India	IDBI was a Central Govt. company for industrial development. Since merged with IDBI Bank.	Permitted under Section 11(5) Not Speculative	

Even investment in land which is not linked to the aims and objectives of the organisation can be deemed to be a speculative investment under Rule 4b.

Chapter XIV

Project Planning & Implementation Risk

Planning! Ah, yes, we know all about planning. Let's skip this chapter and jump to the next.

Indeed, we all know about planning – having used some degree of it at some point in time or other. The typical reaction in the first line of this chapter could be easily forgiven if coming from some corporate executive, as planning and implementation should be second nature to them. To the leadership/management of the NGO, planning is a very, very different (and difficult) ball-game altogether. Planning for a project (or planning for anything) isn't as easy as you think.

> That eminent management guru – Peter Drucker said: *"Strategic planning is the continuous process of making present entrepreneurial (risk-taking) decisions systematically and with the greatest knowledge of their futurity; organizing systematically the efforts needed to carry out these decisions; and measuring the results of these decisions against the expectations through organized, systematic feedback."*
>
> (Source: https://www.azquotes.com/author/4147-Peter_Drucker/tag/risk)

Peter Drucker was talking about strategic planning – something most applicable to the corporate entity and even for such an entity, planning ain't a walk in the park. Planning and implementation are damned hard work. Drucker's quote is quite tough to decipher for the NGO mind, so let's take a look at a less complex one.

> *"Vision is easy. It's so easy to just point to the bleachers and say I'm going to hit one over there. What's hard is saying, OK, how do I do that? What are the specific programmes, what are the commitments, what are the resources, what are the processes we need in play to go implement the vision, turn it into a working model that people follow every day in the enterprise. That's hard work."*

> **– Lou Gerstner**

(Source: https://www.azquotes.com/author/5452-Lou_Gerstner)

What Lou Gerstner essentially describes, in his words, is the act and process of 'planning'. He begins by saying 'vision is easy' and it is – much like daydreaming! As the head/leadership of the NGO it's quite easy to churn out some grandiose dream of what you would like to achieve in a particular period of time. It's easy to say "We are going to do this…." such as 'Eradicate poverty' or 'end hunger' or 'educate street children' or whatever. Vision largely runs on impulse – impulse which is spawned from being witness to some harsh reality.

Yet, mere vision (or dreaming or impulse) doesn't translate into achievement. The people who will (or do) work with you cannot be told 'this is the vision' and they will hit the road and achieve it. Oh, how I wish this was the reality, then life as a leader/manager would be oh so simple and utopian. Communicate the vision to the team and then hit beaches of Goa with a six-pack of beer – that would be the life. Utopia – a figment of human imagination!

Communication of a vision does not equal achievement of the vision because vision is the 'what' part of any plan/intention, the next and more important part being the 'HOW' do we achieve that vision. Gerstner puts this in simple terms very nicely by asking about the programmes, processes, resources, etc which will be required. All these then need to be compiled into one big model or method or plan for the team to follow, towards achieving what we set out to do.

Peter Drucker defined planning (or strategic planning) in detail, by saying that it is a 'continuing' process of making decisions in a systematic manner with the best of knowledge about the future of such decisions and then proceeding to organize in a systematic manner the efforts (processes, resources, programs, etc) to implement these decisions. A secondary part of the planning (and implementation) process is obtaining systematic feedback in order to measure that which has been achieved against that which should have been achieved based on the decisions taken.

It is very interesting to note that Drucker has used <u>one word three times</u> (or it's derivative) in his quote on planning – the word 'systematic' and that, my friends, is the foundation stone or corner stone of planning – doing things *systematically*.

And that brings us to crux of this very problem of planning for the majority of NGOs. In most cases when we plan, we do so on ad-hoc basis or thoroughly unsystematically. **Some of the common pitfalls** in the planning process (if I may call it a process) in NGOs are as follows,

<u>Impulse Project commencement</u> – This author has been witness to many well-meaning projects crashing & burning because they were started on an impulse. Never implement a project purely on the basis of 'vision' – it is the equivalent of venturing into something 'eyes wide shut'. A common mistake we all make is some potential donor comes along and witnesses the good work our NGO is doing and asks us how they can help. Out pops x or y project, which is on our visionary wish-list and pat follows the question "how much do you need to get x project off the ground?". What follows is random estimate (in dollars) plucked from thin air, followed by a commitment to send the money by so-and-so date. And that is how the project cookie crumbles – even before it gets off the ground.

<u>Money matters</u> – Invariably when it comes to planning for a project or programme, we don't seem to get hook, line & sinker into reliable cost projections. Unqualified, inexperienced people provide cost estimates

on anything and everything while planning. For example, someone without an engineer's degree will estimate the cost of constructing a building or will provide an estimate on how much it will cost to feed one child per day or will provide an estimate on the cost of educating one child per month – all estimates being pulled from a magician's top hat!

Planning to plan – This is a particularly lovely one – we always plan to plan; we never plan in order to implement. Another of the brain-busting ridiculous things this author has seen is how, in meetings, we make plans to plan for some project/programme. It gets 'minuted' and that is that. We have planned to plan, so let us pat ourselves on the back and return to basking on the beach in the utopian sun.

Paper planning – In the rare case that we actually spend time planning in some reasonable detail, the plan remains only on paper. When it comes to the implementation, this gets done as per the perspective and choice of the 'man on the ground'. For those of you who remember the comic version of the acronym for the school subject of S.U.P.W., this version of SUPW would mean "Some Useful Paper Wasted".

Narrow perspective – Even when we do plan and the plan is not just a paper-plan but gets implemented, one major shortcoming lies in the narrow perspective with which such planning has been done. For example, a plan developed for a special event such as a seminar or annual school play, is made without getting into the details on 'marketing' the seminar/play to potential candidates or other schools or the public to sell tickets; nor is there an 'advertising plan' nor a detailed fund raising plan; nor a proper budgeting plan, and so on. For a plan to be a proper plan it needs to be holistic in its consideration and not drawn up with a narrow perspective – it needs to encompass ALL aspects relating to the programme being planned for.

No deadlines – In the achievement of anything, time is of the essence. Even a simple plan at the beginning of the day such as "I will eat lunch" requires the specification of a timeline. Obviously, one cannot eat lunch at 7 p.m. and therefore, the plan should also contain a deadline as in "I will eat lunch by 3 p.m.". Similarly, when we plan, we must specify timelines/deadlines by which a particular part of the plan will be achieved. This will enable us to measure in the near future whether that part of the plan has been achieved within the timeline specified or not.

<u>No role assignment</u> – A plan without pre-specified responsibility assigned to specific people is no plan at all. Such a plan assumes that 'everybody will do everything' and in reality, translates into <u>nobody will do anything</u>. Different parts of a plan must be assigned to different people in the team to achieve – all of it cannot be centred on one person alone. For example – marketing assigned to one person, finances (incl. expenditure control) assigned to someone else, fund raising to someone else, etc. Role assignment in the planning process ensures 'load-sharing' and 'distributed accountability'.

Whatever the programme or project, when planning, always hark back to the key word used by Drucker – systematic, systematic, systematic.

With that, let's take a look at some project planning & implementation procedures that we need to keep in mind.

✓ **The vision (WHAT):** As discussed earlier, the vision represents the 'what' part of the planning process and is the very start of everything. "What do we want to do?" is the question that must be asked right in the beginning. The 'what' represents a particular social need that requires addressing or even the reason for the project/programme. The answer to this question will define the broad contours and boundaries of the planning process and even the implementation of the plan. Write down the vision in clear and simple terms, without making it too 'all-encompassing' or 'too unachievable'. As part of the vision try and specify an end timeline by which it should be achieved or by which time, a comprehensive review on the project or programme would be done to establish its longevity, efficacy and sustainability.

✓ **The 'WHY':** Once you have the broad contours of 'what' is being planned, proceed to the 'why'. Why is that social need there? There has to be an underlying cause for the need which has been identified by the vision or the 'what'. The bewilderment over the what & why is quite understandable, so let's take a simple example. Let's say the 'what' is providing a mid-day meal to poor students. The obvious reason for providing the food to these poor students would be that they are hungry or they (their parents) don't have the money to buy food. This of course is the most logical reason.

However, there is a necessity to get deeper into the reason rather than just the prima-facie logical reason. This is done by using a procedure called 'Root-cause analysis'. Root cause analysis is a methodology, normally used in engineering problem solving, for ascertaining the real reason (or root cause) for a problem. In other words, it goes beyond the obvious and focuses on possible reasons which lie at the real root of the problem. In the example, a possible root cause would be that the parents are unemployed or the family's income is insufficient for providing enough food for all the family members. A still deeper root cause could be the father is not skilled or qualified to hold a job or may be unemployed due to a serious economic recession. One of these two could be what is known as the actual/main root cause of the problem. Record the root-cause-analysis on paper as part of the planning process.

It is important to conduct a root-cause-analysis, not just to identify the real root of the problem but more importantly *to ascertain whether the vision will provide a permanent solution to the problem/ social need and whether or not it requires a multi-pronged approach to the problem.* It will also establish whether the approach to the problem requires a short-term initiative or a long term one – thereby directly impacting the duration of the project/programme.

Having done the root-cause analysis, you will be able to determine whether the prima-facie cause is the real/root cause. In the same mid-day meal example, the primary cause would be the parents' lack of money to buy adequate food for the child/children. Stopping at this primary cause would mean the organisation's vision would be limited to providing the mi-day meal to poor students as long as they are in school – which could range from as much as 14 years to as little as 1 year. However, factoring the root cause of the problem into the organisation's vision might call for an additional objective of imparting skill training to the parent/s, to enable them to earn money and buy food for the children/family. This is the classic toss-up between "feed a man a fish every day for the rest of his life versus teach a man how to catch fish". To this author, the latter is the better choice in the medium to long term, on account of it reducing the organisation's financial burden as well as achieving the primary objective – a sort of 'kill many birds with one stone' tactic.

✓ **List the Processes & resources:** Whether the organisation's think-tank/ strategy team decides to run with the primary objective or multiple objectives, the next step is to define in greater detail the processes or steps and the resources which will be required to achieve the vision. With the mid-day meal programme these processes/resources could be a) identifying the school/s for the programme; (b) identifying the 'poor' students; (c) location of the kitchen; (d) requirement of staff; (e) purchasing of food and related items; (f) cooking process and quality management; (g) funding; (h) logistics, etc.

If the vision has been expanded to include skill training for the parent/s, then the processes & resources required in this additional objective would need to be listed separately.

✓ **The 'HOW':** Having established the what, the why and the processes and resources needed, it is now time to get down to the actual nitty-gritty of planning. The 'how' represents the method by which we are going to achieve the vision or the macro-objective. Having split the main objective or vision into multiple processes which will end up contributing to the achievement of the vision, we need to define *targets or micro-objectives/sub-objectives* for each process involved.

These micro/sub-objectives are the key variables in what I call the '*vision achievement equation*'. If you remember middle school algebra (equation "$a = x + y + z...$"), the achievement of the vision or the macro-objective ('a') can be summed up in similar terms as being the sum of the micro-objectives (x, y, z, etc), which are the variables in the equation. To put this in a simpler form, the '*vision achievement equation*' would be as follows.

Vision achievement = Achievement of sub-objective in Process 1 +

Achievement of sub-objective in Process 2 +

Achievement of sub-objective in Process 3 +

Achievement of sub-objective in Process 4 + ...

In the example for the mid-day meal programme the targets or sub-objectives could be as follows.

For a) identifying the school/s for the programme –

Define the criteria for identifying the schools by x date

Provision of mid-day meals to poor children in 5 schools within 6 months of commencement of programme

Provision of mid-day meals to poor children in 10 more schools within 3 years of commencement of programme

For (b) identifying the 'poor' students –

Define the criteria for identifying poor students by y date

Identify 500 poor students (as per the criteria) in the 5 schools within 3 months of commencement of programme

Identify additional 1000 poor students (as per the criteria) in the additional 10 schools within 3 years of commencement of programme

For (c) location of the kitchen –

> Decide by xx date on whether to adopt separate kitchens in each school or use hub-and-spokes system (central kitchen)

> Based on above decision, to further decide the location for central kitchen (if any) and kitchen dimensions

This process of determining the sub-objectives will continue for each process.

✓ **Process Planning** – Thus far we have defined our primary target (or multiple targets) and the processes which will go into achieving the primary target, as well as the sub-objectives for each process. It's now time to get in-depth into each process and plan each process in full detail – similar to an architect developing the contours of each room in a building, the flooring, utilities, the colour of paint, furniture, etc. We will need to decide, in full detail, is what will be done in each process, how it will be done & by when – with derived timelines from the overall project deadline/sub-objectives. In the building example, how the walls will be built (bricks/pre-fab, etc), with what type of bricks, which wall will be built first, how many bricks, cost per brick, cost of cement and sand, number of labourers required, man-hours required per room, cost of labour per man-hour, colour of paint, amount of paint needed, cost of paint per litre, man-hours needed for painting, and so on and so forth. While the building example is a rather detailed one, it would be applicable if you are constructing the building yourself. However, in most scenarios, this job would be handed to a building contractor, in which case it would be wiser to obtain the services of an architect or civil engineer to develop a BOQ or Bill of quantities for you, for the construction.

There are some basic things to keep in mind during process planning. Walk through each process in your mind. Process planning should never be done by one individual alone but by three or four people, each of whom should be logical in their thought processes.

An excellent corporate concept to apply during process planning is the use of CFTs (Cross Functional Teams) – a practice which this author advocates. What are CFTs? CFTs are basically teams of people drawn from the different functions or streams of work in the organisation. In a manufacturing setup, a typical CFT would consist of people drawn from engineering, purchases, manufacturing, finance, administration, possibly HR, etc. Each of these people would bring their individual functional expertise to the table when any issue is discussed or decided. The decision/plan by a CFT results in the plan being (i) broad-based, (ii) holistic in terms of addressing multi-functional issues from the start, (iii) having the buy-in of all the members of the CFT, thereby making the implementation of the plan/decision that much smoother and easier. A decision by a non-CFT could lead to one function/team raising an objection mid-way through the implementation of a crucial project decision, which may stall/delay the implementation and the project.

Each process needs to be examined for whether the implementation of that process will be in one phase or a number of phases spread over the duration of the project/programme. Whether single phase or multi-phase, specify the timelines for each and every activity which require to be completed before the next activity can take place. If the walls of a room do not have bricks in place affixed with mortar, the wall won't be complete and hence can't be plastered and therefore can't be painted. A brief idea of process planning with timelines can be obtained by looking at the sample provided in Annexure I at the end of this book.

Also remember to play the 'numbers game' while planning each process. As far as possible – quantify, quantify, quantify. Process objectives, parameters, costs, etc must be measurable and quantified in terms of time, quantity and/or financial value. Wherever there is a need for a number estimate be objective about it. Do not be subjective and apply your own top-of-the-head estimates but obtain realistic numbers from people in that line of work. A brief idea of numerical estimates can be obtained by looking at the sample programme budget provided in Annexure II at the end of this book, wherein process-wise a few numbers have been defined.

✓ **Job responsibility** – Let's step back and take a breath, since most of the 'heavy hitting' in the planning process has been done. It's now time to assign the responsibility for each process to different people. Those people should be deemed capable (both qualified and able) to fulfil that job responsibility. *Merely picking someone who is the convenient choice or the political consensus candidate will not do.* A project or programme can be consigned to Hades even before its commencement, by assigning a non-capable person to a job-responsibility.

You may designate the person as the process coordinator or team lead (x process) or Director (x process) or whatever nomenclature you wish to allot. The bottom-line is that particular process is a particular person's 'baby' from now till completion of the project or fulfilment of the process responsibility. This individual will be solely responsible for achievement of that process and will be subjected to the 'axe' for non-achievement. Make no mistake, wielding the axe for non-performance is critical because of the *'vision achievement equation'* – where failure to achieve one sub-objective could endanger the overall achievement of the vision.

✓ **Budgeting** – In the process planning stage, the programme has already been planned in great detail, so far as – 'what will be done in each process, how it will be done & by when' as well as accounting for man-hours, quantity of different resources (e.g. paint/bricks/furniture, etc). These numbers will now feed into the programme budgeting directly. If the details have been put into an MS Excel file, you need to add a rate & a total cost column beside the quantity column and add in the formula (Cost = quantity x rate) in the cost column.

The budget for any programme has to be assigned to the Finance person (Finance Director/Finance Controller/Finance Head) of the organisation and to NO ONE ELSE. The Finance guy must not attempt to build/define the budget from the get-go (or start of the planning process) but should build the budget stage by stage. The Finance person (or his one-down) should also be part of every stage of the process planning and also preferably be a member of every CFT. The rationale for this is simple – finance/money is the fuel the program will run on and without it there can be no programme. Even the planning-meetings cost money. The Finance person therefore needs to know every aspect of the programme and when funds are required for what purpose.

While building the programme budget, one must take care to ensure that the costs are worked out according to the implementation phases of the Budget and also the timelines. If there are 5 phases for a programme, then the total cost for each phase and each major item in that phase must be calculated and held on record. Similarly, the total cost based on different timelines must also be calculated and held on record. This information will be needed for the process of assessment and MIS when the particular phase or timeline has been achieved – in order to ascertain whether we have achieved the cost budget or exceeded it. Furthermore, when budgeting, ensure to incorporate all possible cost aspects of the planning process into the cost budget, even conveyance cost & paper cost/photocopying costs – in order to avoid nasty shocks in the future on account of some item/s of cost which were not thought of earlier. Also ensure to provide for an item and amount for 'contingencies' in the budget for every phase, since prices of items/resources are prone to fluctuation on daily/weekly/monthly basis. The contingencies budgeted amount should ideally range between 5% to 10% of the budgeted cost – where 5% should be applied for a high value budget and 10% for a low value budget. For a multi-year budget, try and add in a factor of inflation *if possible*.

In the budgeting process, we have thus far focussed only on the cost/expenditure side of the budget. Let's take a look at the revenue/income side of it. Once you have arrived at the total programme/

project cost, we need to think of how to fund these costs – what the sources of funding would be – whether foreign donations/grants or CSR based funds or crowd funding or government grants or individual based local donations, etc. If there are expected to be multiple sources of funding, it is preferable to allocate a percentage to each source. As with the total cost being calculated based on phase & timeline, the funding also must be based on these phases and timelines. Why? Remember the ALM concept from the previous chapter on Investment Risk? Similarly, your expenditure needs to be matched by your inflows (revenue/incomes). In a funds mis-match situation, you will run short of money and you are liable to face a scenario wherein creditors will demand payments for past supply and may refuse to continue supply since you don't have the money to pay for costs already incurred.

For multi-year projects, once you have completed the budgeting, it is advisable to run what this author refers to as *budget simulations*. Take 2 or 3 of the biggest cost items and ascertain whether these are likely to fluctuate a great deal in the years ahead and tweak the price/ rate in a simulated budget or version 2.0 of the budget. By simulation, you can build in cost projections with provisions for multiple scenarios of 'what-ifs', in this manner – a sort of budget A along with backup Budgets B, C & D for the what-if scenarios. Keep this in mind – *"The wise finance man builds his house upon the rock but provides for storms, earthquakes, floods & lightning!!"*

✓ **Tying up the money** – For those who may be familiar with project financing for corporate projects, a rather important term in project finance is 'financial closure'. Don't panic – the word 'closure' does not mean project closure. It is a term used to denote that point in time when commitments have been received from a project's funding agencies/partners (banks, promoters, etc) and conditions prior to drawing down the money for use, have been fulfilled. This is a rather simplistic definition of the term. For your programme/project, building a revenue budget does NOT mean you have the money – it actually means you only have a target (or target source at best).

You need to plan how to get that money by working out whom you will target, how and then implement the plan. Even after implementing the plan, you do not achieve financial closure for your project/programme. Only when you have secured 'written' commitments from donors, government, etc can you actually say you have achieved financial closure. A strong word of caution – do not initiate your project/programme without achieving financial closure first.

For multi-year projects (more than 3 years), you should have financial support commitments available for the first 3 years (if not more) and have a plan ready to tap more donors from year 2 onwards. Do not wait to reach year 3 and then begin scouting for additional donors/funds – the financial tap will run dry and your project is likely to crash and burn.

✓ **Implementation risk** – No matter how well a project is planned, the implementation risk is the greatest de-railing factor. Planning (and budgeting) is all on PAPER! Implementation is the actual getting-down-in-the-dirt-and getting-it-done part of any project/programme. For implementation to get done well it must follow the plan decided upon (phase-wise & as per timelines) with a provision for unforeseen circumstances and the inputs of the planning team, in such circumstances. In most cases where projects fail, the implementation has been shoddy or not with an eye to detail. _Implementation is the method whereby the plan becomes reality_. Faulty method = faulty reality

✓ **Constant monitoring** – No project planning & implementation is complete without constant monitoring. In reality, most monitoring takes the form of verbal Q&A and that's that. _How much work has been completed? Oh, about 75%. Okay, good._ Next item on the agenda.

This is not how monitoring is done. The monitoring stage is where the phase-wise plan and timelines particularly come in handy. If we are dealing with work in Phase 2, monitoring constitutes asking what are the micro-objectives in Phase 2 and by when are they to be achieved and how much has been achieved by now? Are we ahead of schedule, behind schedule or on track? If we are behind schedule, who is responsible for the laxity and why? Similarly, for the cost projections, upto this stage in Phase 2, how much have we spent on x, y, z items and have we over-spent or are we within budget? If we have overspent, by how much and why? Is the over-spending the result of external factors or factors within the control of those providing over-sight to that work?

A part of Constant Monitoring is '*Success Score Tracking*', wherein we introduce a variance analysis method to the timeline achievements and cost achievements. The success score is a percentage which measures the completion level or the cost achievement level against that which has been projected/budgeted for in the planning and budgeting stages. This process enables us to determine our programme achievement levels and take necessary action on parameters where we are behind and even take necessary decisions to correct problems/crises arising.

So, after all this, are we now still failing to plan? Or perhaps planning to plan? Or even 'paper planning'? Or are we finally going to get our planning & implementation right?

The proof of the planning pudding lies in the implementation thereof, and the proof of the implementation pudding lies in the project results.

As you plan and implement, so shall you reap!

Chapter XV

Measuring Achievement, End-Result Mapping & Goal Fulfilment Risk

Philanthropy is not a joke, neither is the achievement of life-changing social impact!

The latter is the primary agenda of most NGOs – the achievement of an end-result which brings about wide reaching social impact and improvement in the quality of life for those in the marginalised sections of society.

We slog, we sweat, we sometimes curse at the nature of the seemingly 'unrewarding and god-forsaken' task in hand, yet we press on. Much like people in the corporate world, we invest our sweat, blood and tears in the achievement of our goals – though without the financial rewards of the corporate sector. Every NGO does good work, some do great work. For us it's more about the goal-achievement and less about the financial rewards. The satisfaction of achieving the goal tends to be greater than financial reward. There is something about the intangible reward of a 'toothy' smile of a poor child for whom a full stomach is his (or her) definition of happiness or the smile of an underprivileged student getting his first salary from a job obtained after a vocational skill training. Sometimes, it's the gushing verbal 'thank you' and the traditional seeking of 'ashirvad' or blessings, which provides the satisfaction. All of these, however, are the touchy-feely or intangible rewards or result-achievement-indicators for us.

The million-dollar question, that begs asking here "is this the way we measure our goal achievement?" Does our statement on goal achievement amount to a touchy-feely paragraph in a newsletter, with a few numbers thrown in for good measure? Out of all the NGOs out there in the country, it is my estimate that more than 90% don't have a meaningful goal achievement measurement system in place. Goals are not quantifiable in numbers and therefore the good work can't be measured in quantifiable terms.

Goal achievement measurement is one crucial area wherein we need to take a leaf out of the corporate book and modify its' use for the better for the NGO sector. Corporates run on what is called 'MIS' or 'management information system' a.k.a. – the numbers game. It's a management tool which measures the achievement of a set of numbers for a particular period against the pre-determined targets or goals for that period.

As a former corporate executive, no greater bane could have existed for the corporate employee than the dreaded MIS in the spreadsheet or Excel file. Daily, weekly, monthly, quarterly, bi-annually and annually – the corporate MIS system is probably the greatest cause of statistical nightmares and stress for the corporate employee. It's used to aggressively drive business from day-to-day.

However, if you strip away the insanity of the target achievement pressure of the MIS, instead of a management information system it's actually more of a 'measurement' information system, which measures where you are vis-à-vis where you wanted to be. It's part of the feedback & corrective decision/action loop.

The Measurement information system – As an NGO, let's not take MIS to the extreme, instead let's use it as a tool and as an enabler to ensure goal/vision achievement. In order to measure our goal achievement, we need to implement an MIS system and in order to do this, we must first quantify our goals along with timelines within which we would like to achieve them. We have already learnt how to do this from the previous chapter of Planning & Implementation - in the process planning part. Therefore, go ahead and define your own set of numbers for your organisation along with achievement timelines. If you have already completed part of the year or mid-way through a project, do not pick a Herculean target for the short term (say year-end). Doing so, would only demoralize you (and the troops) at year end when the achievement measurement is done and it would serve to defeat the real purpose of the MIS. Use a 'step-up' targeting system – which is essentially setting lower to moderate targets for the present and higher/increasing targets for future, to ensure the overall goal is achieved.

Try and avoid using what I call a 'half baked' MIS. A half-baked MIS is one wherein the MIS does not incorporate key information and still measures achievement against a goal/target. A prime example of this is a profitability/net earnings MIS of a department (say in a hospital) which does not factor in the cost of the machines/equipment, apportioned cost of electricity consumed by the department and apportioned cost of common services. A half-baked MIS would show this department to be 'profitable' to the organisation and worthy of applause, whereas it could be seriously loss making and in need of being shut down. When developing an MIS try, as far as possible, to factor in all elements when quantifying the numbers, particularly when it comes to costing. It is always preferable to write down the components that a particular MIS number would include, as this would make it easier for subordinates/others to follow in the future and would ensure that the MIS is standardised and comparable from year-to-year or from one time-period to another.

Once you have quantified the targets as an accurate representation of the goal or where you want to be in a particular timeframe, you need to determine how you will obtain the data which shows the completion or achievement of such targets. For example, if you are targeting the number of students trained in different vocational courses you need to decide whether this information will be obtained on course completion, monthly basis, quarterly basis or annual basis. Similarly, for the hospital department's profitability MIS you need to decide whether this information will be obtained & calculated on monthly basis, quarterly basis or annual basis. The data collection & collation frequency needs to be defined based on the organisation's requirement frequency for such data. If you have a strong computer system wherein such MIS data is readily available at the click of a button, then the extraction of an MIS and formatting of the data is a relatively easy task. Where you are working with 'archaic systems', monthly MIS systems could prove to be too cumbersome, until and unless you introduce robust computer systems for it, or switch to an online reporting app.

Success score tracking – Now that you have the target numbers quantified accurately and the first achievement MIS numbers available, bring the two sets of numbers alongside each other on a spreadsheet. Looking at the data and comparing the target number with the achievement number, one can easily read and understand whether the target has been achieved/not achieved. You can go a step further and add in another column called 'variance', which is the *target number minus the achievement number*. If the result is positive, then you have that much more left to still achieve and this will get carried over to the next measurement period and be added to the target of the next period. If the variance result is negative, it means that the achievement has been more than the target number and this excess achievement will be carried over to the next measurement period and less work will be needed to achieve the target of the next period.

However, a better and simpler measure would be success score tracking (see last portion of the previous chapter). Success score is basically the 'percentage which measures the completion level or the cost achievement level against that which has been projected/budgeted'. This provides an at-a-glance view of how much has been achieved against the target number. Anything less than 100% means the target has NOT been achieved. A success score between 75%–100% means there is a shortfall which must be made up in the next period. A 50%–74% score would mean a serious shortfall and very hard work would be needed to get the previous job completed in the next time period, as well as getting the next period's target achieved on time. If 50% of the work from Phase 2 is pending, then in Phase 3, we would need to achieve the 50% work of Phase 2 which is pending, as well as achieve 100% of the work target for Phase 3. It is absolutely vital, therefore, that success scores do not drop below 80% at all times, as the sizeable pending work from one phase tends to have a damaging domino effect on target achievement in subsequent phases.

Any success score below 50% means the goal achievement on that particular parameter is in dire straits and this becomes what we refer to, in the corporate world, as a *'fire item'*. The very low success score on this parameter has endangered the 'vision achievement equation' and requires immediate and desperate action.

End-result mapping – Let's retrace our steps to the very first line in the beginning of this chapter.

> "Philanthropy is not a joke, neither is the achievement of life-changing social impact!"

As mentioned at the start of this chapter, most NGOs are in the business of the 'achievement of life-changing social impact!' Yet, do we really measure the life-changing social impact that our work brings about?

After the measurement information system and success score tracking procedures in the preceding paragraphs, you would surely be implementing or thinking seriously of implementing these. Great!

However, look back at the previous chapter in 'The Why' section on the part about root-cause analysis. There is the primary cause and then there is the real cause or the root cause. Building an MIS system for the primary cause isn't that difficult because the facts and figures are more readily available to us. The real MIS needed is one to map the achievement of the end-result for the root cause of the problem. End result mapping takes into account the root-cause of a problem and measures achievement in terms of not just the primary cause but also the root cause. Let's look at **a few examples** in our line of work.

Children's education sponsorship – Someone, somewhere pays money for a child to be educated and the NGO either runs a school for this purpose or else sponsors the education of underprivileged/poor children in some school. The primary cause/goal for achievement is the education of a child who otherwise would not have access to education. The root cause behind educating that child is not absence of mere education, it is to provide that child with an opportunity of a better life/career after completion of their education. The prima-facie cause is education of the child whereas the root of the problem lies in the absence of career opportunity, if education were not imparted to the child. The prima facie need for education is education itself but in reality, almost all parents want to educate their children to provide them with the best career opportunities. Education therefore, in this case, becomes the tool or the means to solve the root cause problem. Do we NGOs track this root cause resolution or do we chase the means hoping to achieve the ends, through some factor of assumption? Do we merely track how many sponsored children have been educated? Or, do we track how many sponsored students of your school/programme are holding good jobs (earning a minimum 'x' amount per annum) or running successful businesses? Tracking the latter is the true "end-result mapping".

Poverty alleviation program – Similarly the primary cause/target for such a programme might be ensuring the person/family is above the poverty line or the family is APL (Above the Poverty Line). The achievement of the primary goal would be whether the person/family is APL or still BPL (below the poverty line). The real root cause, however, behind the poverty could be lack of employment or the main bread-winner being untrained or simply not looking for a job. The being untrained/lack of employment root causes could be treated by vocational training and self-employment. By mapping the BPL people who have been moved to APL category through vocational training and self-employment is actual end-result mapping (or root-cause satisfaction).

Don't just provide for something, ensure its continuity. NGOs are not in the short-term business. We are in the business of 'medium term effect, long term impact'. But we need to measure the long-term impact – which is the real long-term social impact that our work has on society. The end result mapping is NOT short term or even medium-term assessment but measurement of long-term impact.

Goal Fulfilment Donor Risk – While most NGOs don't have tracking or monitoring systems, we fail to realise the risk/s we are running by not having a strong MIS system. Mistakenly, we continue to operate in the belief that our donors will continue sending money till Judgement Day, even with the sketchy reports we provide and we assume they are content with the touchy-feely paragraphs in a newsletter. Philanthropy and fund raising for social sectors, today, is big business – make no mistake about it. There is tremendous competition between donation raising agencies, today. To make matters more difficult, donors across the world and in India are increasingly aware of what results they want to see, for their donations. The intangible and the touchy feely doesn't cut it any more with them. A donor for child education sponsorship wants to see the child's education result – not once a year – but semester-wise, what subjects the child is studying, the living environment, the parents, awards won, holistic child development, etc.

It is vital for your donor to know whether the goal has been achieved or not, or is being achieved and how much. If the donor does not know, the donor will not be satisfied and will shift to some other agency pursuing a similar purpose but rendering strong MIS. Your risk of not having a strong MIS and goal fulfilment tracking can result in 'donor risk'.

Keep up the good work, track your achievements, let your donors/ supporters and well-wishers know.

Chapter XVI

Documentation Risk

Our office processes today are steadily migrating towards paperless systems or 'e-paper' mode of functioning. The fact of the matter, however, is totally paperless systems cannot be a reality and the world over, we will be better off looking to move to 'less-paper' instead of a 'paper-less' style of functioning. There are far too many variables to manage in the 'paperless-migration-journey'. Man has used paper for centuries – from papyrus to actual paper – and will continue to do so for years to come. Many corporates have evolved processes to move away from paper-based functioning given the cost factor, storage factor and maintenance factor, etc. The presence of paper, however, remains.

There are many highly skilled managers whose comparison to 'whiz-kids' or 'hot-shots' in their field of work, would not be amiss. Yet, every Achilles has a 'heel'. Some of the best managers don't seem to have a grip on how to manage 'paper' – ending up at sea with the quantum of paper generated by the organisation. Is your work-desk littered with paper documents or files? Do you spend minutes every now and then shuffling through reams of paper, searching for one document, or do you perhaps have common sets of documents stuffed into transparent plastic folders stacked on the table? You can be the best in your field of technology, finance, banking, manufacturing, education and whatever, yet your inability to tame the 'beast-of-paper' could be your undoing.

In almost two decades of my work-life, across six organisations (corporate & NGO), I have seen good managers unable to come to grips with the volumes of paper (read as 'documentation') in the course of day to day work. I have seen good people put in hours of extra work (at the cost of personal health) just to keep up – with the net result of 'burnout' and mental stress. The inability to properly handle the documentation requirement (and risk) in an organisation can be the undoing of the entity and its manager/leader. I say this not as some 'documentation-guru' born with divine knowledge, nor did it dawn on me with a Newtonian apple falling on my head! Rather, the importance of documentation has been the result of years of experience and learning (which by the way isn't over by a long shot).

My early 'education' on the importance of managing paper/documentation came from my late father (Horace), whose meticulousness regarding paper records was unparalleled. Coupled with a penchant for perfection, his documentation standards were extremely high to live up to. e,g. – documents (including court papers) filed case-wise, chronologically, multiple drafts followed by final versions, with courier slips/registered post acknowledgements, affidavits, counter affidavits, etc. The old man would have beaten a librarian at the librarian's own game.

Contrast this with a visit (in India) to a lawyer's chamber, a government office/record room and I'm truly appalled at how anyone manages to find anything there.

Some years later, when I was working for (erstwhile) Global Trust Bank, Kolkata, I happened to be witness to the regional boss-man literally blow a management trainee (MT) out of the water for improper filing of papers. The said MT had taken an important piece of paper, folded it in half, punched it and filed it – still in half – with the contents not visible. What a tongue lashing the MT got!!

Some 4–5 years later, I got a booster dose of paper managing/documentation process, in HDFC Bank Ltd., with the bank's Service Quality (SQ) Audit and Six Sigma process. You were educated on how to label files, store documents, affix numbers on cupboards and shelves, have indexes to quickly locate papers you need (in seconds, not minutes), etc. Thankfully, I have been able to utilize all these experiential learnings to good effect in the last 10 years – from labelling

& maintaining original Audited Annual accounts from the 1960s to 2018, other crucial documents, and so on.

How do documentation standards in the corporate world have a bearing on the social sector?

There are a great many NGOs who do excellent work in the social sphere but many are pathetic at record keeping. Many decisions are verbal (undocumented), procedures are not written and therefore need to be remembered/revisited each time. A good number of socially successful NGOs find themselves staring down the barrel of the legal gun for want of evidence to submit in a court of law, simply because the relevant documents can't be found or have been misplaced or were never made.

For example – purchase orders made verbally, appointment of staff on verbal basis without appointment letters, and so on.

Our documentation processes need to be strong, simply because the right things in the right place make it easy to find. It also saves time – you spend seconds or at worst a few minutes looking for a document. Importantly a solid documentation system brings order to chaos, directly translating into organisational efficiency. Well maintained records systems also provide for a strong paper trail or audit trail in case of back-checking being necessary and a strong documentary support in compliance & legal cases. The flip side to a strong documentation maintenance process is that it requires storage space and the use of too much paper costs too much money.

Across any typical NGO of moderate size, there a number of functional areas for which documents need to be maintained. Some of these are dealt with below.

Entity records – These are essentially the organisation's documents of formation. Whether the entity is formed as a Trust or Society or Section 25 company, it will have these documents. The originals (whether registered Trust Deed, Memorandum & Articles and Bye-laws, Societies Registration Certificate, Charity Commissioner's certificate, etc) must be held in safe custody by one responsible person – preferably the Managing Trustee/Chairman/Secretary/Managing Director. Photocopies of such crucial documents should be maintained in ready reference files for usage from time to time. Original documents should be used only as and when needed and not handled on a day to day basis.

For schools/colleges/medical colleges, the original Certificate of Affiliation or the registration/permission letter/certificate to carry out instruction in a particular course for colleges, should be included in Entity records.

Also included in the set of entity records would be Photo ID proof & Address proof documents of the Trustees, Managing Committee/Governing body or Board members.

Employee records – This functional area of documentation begins even before an employee can join. If the NGO issues an advertisement in the newspapers or recruits a person through a job consultancy or head hunter, then the copy of the advertisement or contract letter to such consultant should be maintained in a separate 'Recruitment process' file. The reason for this documentation is simple – to avoid accusations of nepotism or lack of transparency etc. If information is circulated only through a particular community, then a copy of letter/s to the community elder/s or heads should be kept on record or some other document which provides similar proof of transparency.

Biodata or CVs received in response to the advertisement should be held in a separate file. Interview call letters, interview result sheets, shortlists, etc should also be held in this file.

Once a candidate is selected, the approval from the relevant approving authority should be placed on record. Thereafter the calculation of the starting salary must be done and the employee's file begun with this calculation document and the biodata.

The appointment letter should be issued in triplicate with one copy being filed in a common employees file and the original plus an employee copy being handed over to the employee. The employee has to sign the original as an acceptance (appointment letter to contain a line stating this) and return this to the employer. This acceptance, though seemingly innocuous, has a very deep legal significance. The employer-employee relationship is in the nature of a 'contract' governed by principles laid down in the Indian Contract Act 1872. The offer (appointment letter or offer letter) containing the mentioned 'consideration' or salary must be communicated to or handed to the prospective employee who needs to read it and accept the offer, for the contract of employment to be complete & in force. Once the candidate signs the letter and returns it, and joins, he/she becomes an employee of the organisation. The accepted offer/ appointment letter must be filed in the employee file.

The new employee must also provide other documents such as copies of educational and professional qualifications, copies of work experience letters (appointment letters, resignation letters, release letters) from previous organisations worked for, as well as copies of previous salary slips, ID proof, address proof, etc. These documents should be verified with originals before placing them in the employee file. *It is always preferable to arrange for a verification check on qualifications & experience claims of a new employee, as falsification of credentials is more easily done than is expected.* Once an employee has joined, a detailed job-description should be provided to the person and a receipted copy placed in the employee file for reference. In the course of the employee's tenure, different letters may be issued for contract renewal, for probation or confirmation as permanent employee, for any salary revisions, promotions, employee leave requests, other employee request, general employee notices, etc, all of which need to be filed in the employee's file. Additionally, a copy of the employee's gratuity nomination form should be filed here too.

In certain cases, letters may be issued for disciplinary reasons and show-causes, etc. These must be kept in the employee file, as well as the employee's written responses in such matters. Any retirement letter issued before retirement should also find its way into the employee's file. The same applies for resignations and termination of service. In an employee-death-case, the copy of the employee's death certificate must be filed in the employee file after due verification with original and certification of the same.

At the end of an employee's tenure with an organisation, the employee file must look like a complete dossier on the employee's employment history with the organisation.

On a separate note, the NGO must also maintain separate files for Salary scales and job descriptions for various job roles. Additionally, there must be well-documented policies for promotions/increments for people acquiring a particular skill which relates to a job role they are in; as well as increments/incentives for employees attaining higher educational/professional qualifications (e.g. Graduation/MBA or X degree) in their relevant field of work.

Accounting records – No NGO can function without having finances to work with and consequently where there is money (public money, that is), there is a need to account for it. Hence accounting records must be maintained for money received and spent.

The accounting records list begins with the custody of the entity's Permanent Account number (PAN card and letter), TAN number and letter, the organisation's registration certificate under section 12A & 12AA of the Income Tax Act, the FCRA registration certificate (new & old), etc. Though these original documents may be classified as entity records, they are primarily finance documents and their custody should be with the Finance department as these tend to be required more often than the other entity records.

Among the day to day documents are the original bills (whether utility bills, suppliers' bills, miscellaneous bills, etc) which are received for payment in due course. Once payment has been made against a bill, a voucher (generated by software or a hand-written one) needs to be attached with the bill and filed separately. Bills may be filed utility-wise or vendor-wise or payment-mode-wise – though the filing must be in chronological order.

Every accounting dept., will necessarily be dealing with employee payroll. Payslip counterfoils should be maintained in hard-copy or scan-copy for quite a lengthy period of time, as these can prove to be critical in cases of employee litigation.

At the end of a specific time period (month/quarter/year) printouts of the ledgers must be maintained in a separate file. For NGOs which adopt e-payment systems such as RTGS/NEFT, the records for these (whether single transaction at a time or multiple) must be retained in a separate bank file complete with the bank statements. This needs to be done to enable an easy matching of transactions requested versus transactions actually carried out, as part of a Bank reconciliation process.

Original audited accounts of the organisation should be maintained year-wise in separate files, with photocopies in ready access folders.

Accounting records generally consume the most storage space but their maintenance is crucial.

Documentation risks under the accounting setup do not just pertain to maintaining documents. There are risks which arise from not exercising due diligence and not following basic logical processes. Some of these risks are listed below.

- Payments made on the basis of scan copies of bills and original bill not obtained. Documentation risk takes the form of the *same bill being paid twice* – once on photocopy/scan copy and again on the original.

- Original rent receipts not submitted but payment made on photocopy or on declaration.

- Rent agreement not submitted for authenticity – risk is the property being rented may not exist or fraudulent rent receipt is produced to claim reimbursement.

- Medical benevolence paid against copies of bills – risk is the beneficiary can claim benevolence support from multiple organisations

- Falsified medical bills – The employee may have a medical reimbursement allowance and against this, bills are produced from a medical store which also supplies general goods. The employee (or family member) may not be a cardiac patient but bills for high priced cardiac medicines are submitted to claim reimbursement.

Statutory compliance records – A few chapters ago, we dealt with compliance & legal risks and this aspect is a continuation of that. Compliance with statutory provisions is the first (and major) part of the pie – maintaining the documents/records for it is the second part. In the event of a systems failure or claim by a government body for alleged statutory non-compliance, you will end up receiving the wrong end of the stick if documents in your defence are missing or just not available. Your defence will amount to merely 'your word against that of the government' and we all know the outcome of such a defence.

Key statutory documents such as registration certificates or letters for Provident Fund, Employee State Insurance, Profession Tax, Registrar of Societies, etc need to be held in safe custody, with photocopies available for daily use.

When PF/ESI/PTax calculations are made copies of these calculations must be held on record along with the payment proof (paid challan printouts). Copies of returns filed under Income Tax, etc must be held on record for future reference. Such documentary proof may never be required but if it ever is, the absence of the document can prove unbelievably damaging.

Process records – These records are the direct result of operational procedures mentioned in the earlier chapter on operational risk. Once you have a Standard Operational Procedure (SOP) in place, processes must follow accordingly and the documents generated from such procedures need to be filed as evidence of procedures followed.

For example, in the laid down process for purchases documentation the requirements could be quotations, rates and rate comparisons, selection of final supplier, approval on record, purchase order issued, delivery challan with receiving for materials received, invoice for goods supplied and billed for.

For non-supplies or large building contract orders, the documentation requirements could be Bill of Quantities (BOQ), tendering and bidding process including Earnest Money, selection of L1 bidder, approval from apex body or approving body as per delegation of powers (DoP), issue of work order, etc.

Once the organisation's SOP has been defined, the list of process documents which are necessary (to evidence completeness of a process) should also be drawn up and adhered to. The process can then be subject to a 'process audit' on annual or bi-annual basis.

Record of Meetings & approvals – Each and every NGO must have periodic meetings of its Trustees, Governing body or Board or Apex body, in order to decide on various matters that fall within their jurisdiction and to decide on policy and future strategy. Such meetings are absolutely critical as these may be meetings to decide the road ahead or wrestle with problems/crises facing the organisation or approve or decline other decisions placed before them. Hence the documentation accorded to such meetings takes on a huge significance. Such decisions can also be subject to scrutiny by external regulatory bodies and/or the government/courts and hence great care must be taken when recording the minutes and decisions of such meetings.

There are a number of aspects that should be looked into when minutes of the meeting are recorded. Some of the basic ones are as follows.

i. *Recording secretary* – This role is distinct and different from the 'Secretary' of the organisation. The recording secretary is someone who has a very good command over English or the language in which the minutes will be recorded and is someone who is deemed to be fully trustworthy (and not a 'blabbermouth'). He/she should have a good memory and also know short-hand or else be very quick in making notes in 'long-hand'. An additional skill, the person should possess, is the skill to summarize and the sensibility to filter out unnecessary words/ comments of discussions when finalizing the draft minutes of the meeting. To clarify – a discussion point with 25 paragraphs in 'long-hand' should not be reproduced verbatim but summarized to 2 paragraphs at best plus 2–3 lines to record the final decision/ resolution.

ii. *Secretary* – The Secretary of the organisation is the officer/person appointed as such, with the powers, authority and responsibilities as defined in the organisation's byelaws/Memorandum and Articles. The Secretary is also the person who is responsible for affixing his/her signature to the final minutes of the meeting – minutes which become an official document/record of the proceedings of the meeting/s.

iii. *Quorum* – Quorum simply refers to the minimum number of members (out of the total) that are required to attend for a meeting to be considered valid and to accord an authenticity/ sanctity to its decisions. For example – for a Board of 10 members, if a minimum 7 members are required to attend then if only 6 are present for a meeting, the meeting cannot be held and even if held, decisions taken at such a meeting will be deemed invalid for lack of quorum. The criteria (number of members required) for a quorum for different types of meetings is usually included in the organisation's byelaws/Memorandum and Articles. *It is absolutely critical that the minutes of the meeting record the names of those present at the meeting AND clearly mention that quorum has been obtained* or that the quorum criteria for such meeting has been established. In the absence of a line to this effect, a meeting can be deemed infructuous (without any purpose or value – source: Cambridge dictionary) and decisions taken in such meeting can be held invalid. The invalidation of a past meeting and its decisions can have far reaching ramifications and disastrous consequences for the organisation.

iv. *Partial attendance at meetings* – There are often situations where members attend meetings at the beginning but one or two may need to leave during the course of the meeting due to personal exigencies. The minutes of the meeting should record the time of departure of the member leaving during the meeting. This is important, since during any litigation (i.e. court case/regulatory proceedings) at any future stage, a member may state that he/ she was not present when that decision was taken and absolve themselves of individual responsibility. It is also the duty of the Secretary/Convenor or chairman of the meeting to note the departure and ensure that quorum is not lost due to 1 or 2 members leaving mid-meeting. *With a member leaving mid-meeting if quorum is lost, then the meeting thereafter ceases to have its procedural sanctity and its authority.* This may be avoided if the Byelaws/Memorandum and Articles provide for validity of a meeting even if quorum is lost mid-meeting due to one or two members needing to leave for pre-specified reasons and the permission of the convenor/chairman is received for the same. This should not apply to cases where some members stage a 'walk-out' from a meeting.

v. *Start & end timing* – The minutes should preferably also record the time the meeting started and ended. While not critical, it is advisable merely as a precaution.

vi. *Approvals as per DoP* – The minutes of a meeting should ensure adherence to the organisation's Delegation of Powers (DoP) matrix. In other words, the minutes of the meeting for a committee (with only recommending powers) should only record the suitability of a proposal/matter and contain recommendations of the same to the next higher body for approval/consideration. Recording as 'approved' an agenda item for such a committee could amount to non-adherence with the DoP.

vii. *Approvals by circulation* – In today's hectic day and age, members of committees and Boards do not have spare time to meet every week or sometimes even every month. The work of the organisation, however, must not come to a grinding halt merely because members are unable to meet at such frequent intervals. With email facility being available (at the fingertips) to almost all owning a smartphone, background information and resolutions can be circulated to members who can access these 'on-the-go' and reply immediately or in a few days. Such email-based approvals should be held on record and the same resolution tabled in the next meeting (with physical presence of the members), for ratification of the earlier email-based approvals. This author is aware of at least one such organisation which believes in holding all important and moderately important decisions for its apex body in its bi-annual/annual meetings.

viii. *Circulation of minutes* – The minutes of the meeting should be circulated to the members for their record well before the next meeting – either by email or by hard copy. *Emailing minutes to the members a few hours/minutes before the next meeting is a definite no-no*, as this does not provide time to the members to read and analyse the minutes for possible ramifications, corrections, etc.

ix. *Organisation record* – The original copy of the minutes of the meeting must be held on record in a separate file meant for such minutes and not in a 'general documents file'.

x. *Follow-up action* – A part of usual process with meetings and minutes is that certain items get carried forward for actioning, since an immediate decision may not be possible for want of information or an approval may be conditional or require a 'reporting back' to the committee by an individual member on action taken. The recording secretary/secretary/convenor (whoever is authorised) must follow-up with the individual member to ensure that the necessary action-taken-report has been prepared by the member (preferably in writing) for the committee.

Specialised records – There are special sets of records which require to be maintained from time to time.

One of these specialised sets is 'death case documentation'. It is never a pleasant task dealing with demise of an employee – particularly one who has served the organisation for many years. Despite the unpleasantness of a subordinate/colleague's demise, as an employer one must be objective *and cautious* when dealing with the documentation for such cases and when interacting with the next of kin. Death cases can be some of the trickiest documentation cases to deal with and can put an organisation in a 'legal soup' with claims from the next of kin. The basic documents that must be obtained in such cases is found in the Chapter on 'Compliance & Legal risk' under the section Death case gratuity payment & documentation.

The risks inherent in dealing with death cases is when no nomination by the employee (now deceased) is available for gratuity or terminal salary. In the case of a nomination being available, payment can be made after establishing the identity of the nominee/s. Where there is no nomination and there are multiple potential claimants (as next of kin), it is critical for the employer to ask for a succession certificate from a court of law, as a protection against future claims/disputes by the various claimants. It is unwise to play adjudicator in such cases or attempt to share the terminal dues among claimants. The risk here is immense as in the absence of proper legal documents, the organisation can be ordered by a court of law to pay penalties to claimants for terminal dues paid outside the sanctity of law/legal process.

Death case documentation must be maintained (verified copies/originals) in a separate file and employee wise – using plastic separators/dividers.

Be warned to take special care with such documentation, as this author is aware of rather strange (and tricky) cases. One that comes to mind is an employee with 2 wives (separated from one, married to/living with another) with 2 children from the first wife and one from the second wife. Nomination existed in favour of the first wife and then was changed to second wife.

Another example is an employee with one surname, later changes his (including wife & children's) surname – without providing due notice to employer. He also had a second wife. Employee died in a vehicle accident and the death certificate was issued in the new surname!

Legal records – During the course of an organisation's life, it will – beyond a doubt – get dragged to a court of law on some matter or the other, whether as a plaintiff (one filing the case) or as a defendant or merely as a witness/related party to a dispute. Whatever the case may be, a court case will involve correspondence with lawyers, case briefs/initial filing documents (also known as the 'plaint'), certified copies of court documents, orders or judgements, etc. Documents pertaining to one particular case (including draft copies and all relevant documents) should be maintained in one single file or folder relating to that case and the file labelled with the case number. Do not club documents of different cases handled by one lawyer in one file or folder – when the time comes to produce a document to the judge, you do not want to be spending the court's valuable time searching through dozens of papers to find one page.

The same logic applies for separate cases for income tax (cases and appeals), labour commissioner matters, PF and ESI complaints to govt, property disputes, etc. All of these files/records should be held in safe custody with access restricted to a few people only.

Property deeds – Every organisation, from time to time, has the necessity to invest in property (i.e. land and/or buildings) – whether to house its offices, employees, for children's homes, schools, training centres, etc. Such properties are often purchased or taken on lease (rented). Irrespective of the mode (purchase/lease), the transaction will result in a paper document by way of a sale deed or lease agreement, in original. These documents must be held in very safe custody with access to very few people in the organisation. The reason behind such restricted access is that these documents are the ownership/title deeds to the property purchased or the place leased. The loss of a title deed can be quite problematic for the owner and can even result in a fraudulent sale should the original deed fall into the hands of an unscrupulous party.

Original title deeds/lease agreements should preferably be stored in a bank locker after copies of the same have been made for ready reference. If the organisation owns a number of properties, it is advisable to make a list of the properties (i.e. a ready reckoner) with Municipal Corporation assigned assessee numbers, total property size, name of the previous owner, cost of acquisition, storage location of deed, end-use of property, pending works on such property (e.g. boundary wall, mutation, construction, electrification, etc).

There are a few common mistakes organisations make during acquisition/purchase of a property. In the banking industry, prior to sanction of a home loan/mortgage loan, the bank would undertake a title-search of the property records for a minimum of the last 15 years to ensure that there is no encumbrance or defect in the title to such property. This is called a *non-encumbrance certificate* and is obtained from a lawyer after a property records search. Many organisations enter in property deals with 'eyes-wide-shut' only to burn their fingers later and find defective title deeds and disputed properties. This is your documentation risk for inadequate/improper documentation. Obtaining a non-encumbrance certificate is a non-negotiable requirement prior to a property purchase. Furthermore, it is advisable to obtain a search report on the said property for the last 50 (fifty) years and not 15 years simply because 15 years is now too short a reliable time span. For example – a large property may have been sub-divided and sold 40 years ago and some disputed portion still included in a deed made 20 years ago. A 15-year search of the land records may not reveal the defect. Also, property numbers (called 'dag' numbers) can get classified and re-classified with changes in governmental land records changes, changes in state/district boundaries, etc.

Another aspect to look out for is the presence/absence of blue-prints/drawings and sanction plans for buildings on a piece of land to be purchased. For any building on a property, it is important to have an official sanction from the local Municipal Corporation/ Panchayat, etc. A building without such permission/sanction could be considered as an unauthorised construction and liable to be demolished by the authorities. It would cost a lot to have an illegal/ unauthorised building/construction legalised by the authorities, as all manner of official and opportunistic 'unofficial financial requests' would be raised for according the delayed sanction.

Old records retention – For NGOs which are over 10 years old the question of retention of old records arises. Paper records/files take up large amounts of space and accounting records alone can fill up a mid-size room in 10 years. While all records cannot be retained for decades on end (one would need a warehouse), it is important to decide on a documents-retention-policy. Example:

➤ Entity records will be retained indefinitely.

➤ Employee records need to be kept for 10 years after the employee retires/resigns/is terminated.

➤ Accounting records to be retained for 10 years

With the information technology improving by leaps and bounds every year, records can now be stored for a larger number of years with less space than ever before. Old records can be scanned and stored in a high memory capacity computer server or in external hard disks or in DVDs. This mode of retention, if adopted, should also find a mention in the organisation's documents-retention-policy.

- - - - -

More often than not, we NGO types tend to ignore the importance of documentation, till it's too late. The much hated 'blast-from-the-past' catches us on the wrong foot big-time, leaving us wondering why we did not have our documentation procedures in place. Documents retained in one place according to a solid policy, according to well laid down guidelines & procedures can do wonders in such cases. The author remembers a labour case filed by an employee of an organisation pertaining to a matter/emoluments' decision of 1991. The employee had given a very negative spin to the decision based on the employee's old salary slips. Among the 'saving grace' documents for the organisation, was a manual salary register of the 1990s which covered some months before and after the 1991 salary decision was given effect. The employee's false claim went up in smoke.

There is a high degree of potential risk in being lax with documentation – whether documentation not obtained/not maintained or improper documents obtained or even documentation improperly prepared.

As with the other risks, with documentation too, you need to remember –

An ounce of documentation is worth 'pounds' of cure!!

Chapter XVII

Myopia

For the NGO, this is not so much a risk – it's a disease! A disease not of the organization but of the man or men (or even women) in leadership.

Medically, myopia is classified as a vision condition or an eye disorder. However, the myopia referred to here is no medical disorder or condition – it's a disease of the mind and the attitude – whether deliberate or accidental. Whichever the case, the individual's disease can prove to be 'blinding' for the organisation.

Before we look at the truth and consequences of this 'disease', let's look at myopia in the medical sense. While searching for a medical definition of myopia, I found the following on the Mayo Clinic website and just love the way it is described there, in their overview section. The key words applicable to this chapter have been *italicised*.

"Near-sightedness (myopia) is a common vision condition *in which you can see objects near to you clearly, but objects farther away are blurry*. It occurs when the shape of your eye causes light rays to bend (refract) incorrectly, focusing images in front of your retina instead of on your retina."

Again, a little later, under their heading 'When to see a doctor' – the Mayo Clinic writeup reads:

"If your difficulty clearly seeing things that are far away (distance blur) is pronounced enough that you can't perform a task as well as you wish, or if the quality of your vision detracts from your enjoyment of activities,...."

(Source: https://www.mayoclinic.org/diseases-conditions/nearsightedness/symptoms-causes/syc-20375556)

The medical writeup lists a few key things about myopia, which are as follows.

- ☞ You see objects near to you clearly
- ☞ Objects farther away are blurry
- ☞ The distance blur can prevent you from performing a task as well as you wish
- ☞ The quality of detracts from your enjoyment of activities

Many of us suffer from myopia as a medical condition and the above list is true for us, resulting in us wearing corrective lenses (spectacles or contact lenses) or even undergoing specialised surgery. For those of us who are medically myopic, we seek (or have sought) to correct it.

Yet, what of those in leadership, who are myopic (not medically, that is)? What about these individuals, who cannot see clearly?

The first two conditions on the above list are painfully obvious and true for them, yet the tragic truth of it all, is that they are blissfully UNAWARE of the fact that they are myopic leaders. The even greater tragedy occurs when that blissful ignorance (of their myopia) leads to arrogance and obstinacy – the arrogant and obstinate attitude of *"Even though I cannot see, I am NOT blind"*.

Are you laughing? Do you know someone like that in leadership in your NGO?

I cannot help but remember a version of an old quote (from 12th century John Heywood's compilation of proverbs) that my late father, Horace, would often say.

"One can lead a horse to water, twenty cannot make it drink."

To all of us, the first part of the proverb is obvious – it's easy to lead a horse to the water or, in other words to bring it to the water source but a stubborn (obstinate), arrogant "horse" will refuse to 'drink' – even if it is thirsty and even if twenty people try to make it (understand). That proverb is so true of myopic leadership.

Myopic leaders are of largely 3 types: Type A which sees only that which is immediately near not distant. Type B is the 'My will be done' type and, finally, Type C is the Money Power Position type.

Type A Myopic Leaders

These leaders are broadly those who 'cannot see long term'.

They fall into one of 3 sub-categories. First, type (A-1), are those who genuinely don't see distance because they lack the ability to do so. They may have been named as leaders by their organisations but are leaders only in name and not in deed or skill or sense. They do not possess the wherewithal to do what their organisations have called them to do. These are the genuinely long-term blind.

Type A-2 includes leaders are those who see but don't want to see or rather choose not to see. What is obvious to everyone else in the medium to long term, is visible to this bunch also but they prefer to wear scales over their eyes – maybe hoping that the unfavourable portions visible in the distance will become invisible and simply fade from sight. This sub-type 'see but will not see!'

Type A-3 is what I would refer to as the 'scaredy-cat' type, with Leadership phobia. They see short, medium and even long-term reasonably clearly but are fearful of taking action lest the results blow up in their faces, making them accountable to their apex bodies. They secretly value their seat or 'kursi' and do not wish to lose it. This group are afraid of facing the firing squad in the night or the gallows at dawn.

The scaredy-cat leader is so aptly described by Tom Clancy – the well-known author of many espionage novels – in his book 'Red Rabbit', in an unrelated quote – "It's so strange, how much fear there was in the world, and the most fearful of all were so often those who held the power in their hands." (page 53, para 2)

Some just cannot see beyond their noses – beyond personal position and power and how to safeguard it, even at the cost of the future of the very organization which they are called to lead. The scaredy-cat ones like the 'chair' or 'kursi' they are in and don't want to be in the firing line of their apex bodies/ Boards and are all too content maintaining the status quo – even when dynamic & strong leadership is the need of the hour. The love of the chair is greater than the love for the cause!

Myopic leaders, of Type A, see only the here and now, whether it is unintentional and resulting from simple lack of clear 'future vision' or whether it is deliberate. For those for whom it is unintentional, there is still hope – the disorder can be corrected, first by accepting the existence of the disorder and second by adopting corrective measures – much like getting a pair of spectacles. However, it will require some substantial degree of humility!

For Type A-2, the remedy will be nothing short of the scales falling from their eyes. For Type A-3, much like the cowardly lion in Wizard of Oz, it will take a long trip down the yellow-brick road to find their courage and gumption.

Type B Myopic Leaders

These leaders are the ones who subscribe to the 'I will see only my version of long term' school of thought.

All of us have heard of the words "Thy will be done". The Type B myopic leader however is a firm believer in "My will be done". This kind of myopia comes with the philosophy of "I am God in this universe and it's my way or the highway". There is no other opinion or picture that makes a difference to this leader.

Decisions are taken based on an opinion – only one opinion – the myopic leader's opinion, that is.

For this kind of leader, your eye bends the light (or what you see) to show exactly what _you want to see_. It doesn't even show up as a blur. This form of myopia has deep roots in the individual ego – a subscription to the personal motto of "I am right and everyone else is wrong" or at the worst a belief that "Even when I'm not right, I'm never wrong".

This type chooses to see a distorted reality through the defective retina of their eyes.

Type C Myopic Leaders

Type C is the MPP or Money Power Position type and can only see 'their personal long-term gains'.

This, by far, is the worst category of myopic leader. This leader, as the nomenclature suggests, is after money, power or position or ALL three together. He/she is chasing gold with the personal objective of _self-enrichment_ rather than the organisation's objective of social enrichment of others.

The 'Power and position' seekers chase the 'kursi' and employ that major tool called politics to ascend the ladder to the seat/s of power and to stay there. The position brings the power and the power is used to consolidate the position – a kind of chicken and egg story. Much energy is expended by such leader/s to remain in those positions of power – such that there is little steam left in the boiler, for the real work of the NGO.

The fact of the matter is the social sector organisation is the wrong place for chasing gold – money is always in short supply. If you're looking for the proverbial pot of gold, I suggest you try the other side of the rainbow (i.e. the corporate world).

For the power & position gents, I strongly recommend you join the actual world of politics – join Parliament.

- - - - -

What kind of leader are you? The myopic type or the clear-vision type? Do you fall into Type A, Type B or Type C myopic category? Look into the mirror, ask others (but don't ask the 'yes' men) and <u>unto thine own self be true!</u>

If you are myopic, whether by chance or by choice, your myopia will never allow you to plan effectively for the organisation's future, since you cannot see far enough down the road or else your vision is distorted. You can't see the long term clearly and because you can't see far enough, therefore, you can't see the writing on the wall!

You will also lack what I call 'Kerb vision' – or seeing around corners. Superman can see through walls, Spiderman's 'Spidey' sense tingles at the sense of impending danger. Leadership myopia will allow you the benefit of neither.

Whatever the case may be – the last 2 things (out of 4) on the myopia list (at the beginning of this chapter) get fulfilled. The consequences of the myopia would be a) As a leader you don't enjoy the leadership role and b) neither can you fulfil the task you were called to do. In the eyes of your Board/Governing Body/apex body, sooner or later you will be marked down as a failure. After all, time exposes all and irreparably so. When it happens, the scaredy-cat will be confronted with the very reality of their nightmare – that is, the firing squad in the night or the gallows at dawn.

Bottomline – You didn't enjoy your leadership role since you were always busy dodging bullets, or chasing your own pot (or kursi) of gold at the end of the rainbow or you were busy at playing Hitler or Stalin. Worse, you failed in the task as a leader, you're marked as a failure for life – a permanent scar that will follow you to the grave.

I have said this so many times, the NGO world today is dynamic not static as in yesteryear – behold the new order cometh and the old hath passed away.

Much like chess, we need to see far ahead, think ahead and plan at least three moves ahead. We must mentally map the 'road ahead' for the organisations we lead, not follow the road till the next cross-road and then ask for directions. Myopia will not allow us to do any of this.

If you fall into any of the above three myopic leader categories, step aside, get out of the way of your organisation's objectives. Type A leaders – hire a professional and let him (or her) do his job, because it means you don't have the wherewithal (skill-set) to handle specialised work in that particular domain. The professional can and will see better and farther than you can see and as a professional, he will bring to bear a skill-set that will help map the road ahead. The professional, by virtue of his skill and experience, will also empower the myopic scaredy-cat – after all, there is strength in numbers.

Type B & C myopic leaders, just hire a professional and let him (or her) do his job – don't expect them to rubber stamp your wishes or endorse your plans or help in your personal long-term gains. When you hire a professional, the organisation benefits greatly from his skill-set and when the organisation grows and succeeds, as the leader you grow with it.

Myopia is, by far, the greatest risk for any NGO. You may be fantastic in containing/managing/mitigating all the other risks except this.

Myopic leaders are the one risk – rather the gaping hole – which
<u>will</u> sink your ship!

Chapter XVIII

To Risk or De-Risk!

The social sector of late is fast being recognised as the 'third sector' – after the public sector (or government/govt. companies) and the private sector (the business corporate). Yet it is this third sector that provides the crucial plug that fills some of the holes (and deficiencies) left by the first two sectors, in delivery of much needed services. Quality education to poor children, healthcare for the poor, skill training to the unemployed and the school dropout – all these are focus areas for the third sector. Areas where the first sector tries but does not succeed (woefully, so and for a variety of reasons) and the second sector (most of it) could not be bothered, except if there be a business (read 'profit') opportunity in it. The much touted 'trickle-down' effect is in reality just that – it trickles down, years and even decades later.

The reality of it should stare you in the face – the NGO is not just an isolated entity which does good work for the socially downtrodden or exploited ones or the less fortunate. *You are the third sector.*

If I may tweak the introductory lines from Star Trek, these would read.

"The Social sector – the final frontier. These are the voyages of the NGO, it's continuing mission to explore difficult new avenues, to seek out new social challenges and new solutions, to boldly go where no one has gone before..."

For many of the socially downtrodden/exploited/less fortunate, possibly your NGO may be the only chance they have at a better life. The presence, the role and the importance of the third sector is becoming more and more evident with the passage of time. Therefore, what we do in the third sector becomes all the more critical for the country's social upliftment. The risks we undertake become that much more critical as there isn't much of a safety net for the sector.

Before proceeding with the ending, let's go back to the beginning. As I said in the 'Preface', coming from a professional setup to a much less structured NGO environment, it was both appalling and unthinkable, at how casually things could be handled – whether out of ignorance or intentionality. Termination of employment would certainly have been the reward in the corporate world for such a casual approach to business. From a world where operational guidelines and standard operating procedures were common and standardised across hundreds of bank branches across the country, to an environment where operational guidelines were not documented nor were standard operating procedures – even for institutions which were decades old. Do you scramble to write process when you are under the microscope? Or do we subscribe to the 'house on fire, dig a well' policy?

As for planning, the ills of the 'planning' process abound. Planning is a fancy word with little else behind it.

On the one hand, the social sector need is immense and the demands for the remedy of social sector ills is set to expand and expand many times over.

On the other hand, the NGO environment has transitioned from what was a relatively static environment to a highly dynamic one in just a decade. The dynamic content in the sector will not settle – the dust storms will go on. The few entities which have professionals on board will survive and hopefully thrive, others will flounder and even fail.

There is a marked (even, skewed) imbalance between the 'what' needs to be achieved and the 'how' to achieve it. That imbalance sums up the risks facing each and every NGO in the sector. An imbalance that must be corrected or de-risked in order to fulfil/balance the vision achievement equation.

You can begin by first 'RECOGNISING THE RISK', (or risks) which may be applicable to your entity and then correcting the imbalance by 'DE-RISKING'.

This book seeks to high-light and address some of the day-to-day risks faced by NGOs and tries to lay down the foundations for strong NGO management. It is not an exhaustive work, since each NGO has a unique operating environment and to achieve the 'exhaustive' ends, would take many years of research.

The book brings to bear some of my own professional experience and contrast this with NGO experience, not as a critique, but in an endeavour to build a bridge between the two worlds.

"De-risking the NGO" is meant to be an enabler for NGO leadership – to manage better and more effectively, since it is probably the NGO that can reach the grassroot levels of society best.

Plan better, implement better, manage better – achieve more!!

Above all remember:

"Knowledge is power, ignorance is RISK."

Sample Process Planning with Timelines

(indicative & not exhaustive)

Programme objective: Providing mid-day meals to poor students in schools

Root cause: Unemployment/unemployability of parents, hence low family incomes

Solution for achieving primary objective: Provision of mid-day meals to poor students

Solution for root cause problem: Imparting Skill training to parents of poor children

Processes for achievement of Primary objective

1. Identifying schools for Mid-day meal provision programme
2. Identifying poor students for Mid-day meal provision programme
3. Identifying the location for the kitchen for mid-day meal programme
4. Obtaining the kitchen space by purchase/rental
5. Identifying the staff required
6. Recruiting the staff
7. Deciding on other ancillary resources (vegetable contractors/fuel/ transportation)

Programme commencement/go-live target date: 01.06.2020

Process Planning with timelines

	Process Sub-objectives	Phase	Deadline	First Person responsible (FPR)	Completion date	Deadline achieved (Y/N)	If not achieved, reasons for the same	(Author's planning tip)
a.	Define the geographical area & criteria for identifying the schools where programme shall be implemented and identifying the first 5 schools	Phase 1	31.03.2020					Do not plan for a huge area. It is better to start small and continue to scale-up based on one's successes & resource constraints.
b.	Define the criteria for identifying the poor students	Phase 1	15.04.2020					Keep in mind the future scale-up & the fact that demographic patterns change from area to area. The criteria must be inclusive but not too general

c	Decision on separate school kitchens or centralised kitchen	Phase 1	15.04.2020			Keep in mind the future scale-up & ensure that any centralised kitchen is located in a place easily accessible by road or rail, across the target geographical area. This will avoid making relocation changes in future.
d.	Decision on location of centralised kitchen & dimensions and necessary equipment (if centralised kitchen opted for)	Phase 1	15.04.2020			Decide but keep in mind the expansion plan for the medium term future. Do not decide based on today's need but based the requirement 6 months/1 year down-the-line. This will avoid buying new equipment every 6 months.

Continued...

e.	Identifying the staff required	Phase 1	15.04.2020			Identify the requirement for now, 6 months later and one year later
f.	Arrangements for kitchen location/s on rent/purchase (centralised or local)	Phase 1	15.05.2020			
g.	Recruiting the required marketing staff	Phase 1	30.04.2020			Avoid recruiting too many staff
h.	Recruiting the required staff (others)	Phase 1	15.05.2020			Recruit the immediately required staff. After 6 months you can recruit more based on the 6 month requirement plan. If you recruit all at one go, you will end up paying staff for sitting idle for 6 months.

i.	Completion of contact programme with 5 schools & programme-sign-up	Phase 1	15.05.2020			Ensure to have at least one school staff as the contact person & coordinator for the programme
j.	Estimating total food & fuel requirements per day for x number of students	Phase 1	20.05.2020			
k.	Ancillary resources – contracts for food vendors	Phase 1	20.05.2020			Include a clause for increased supply after 6 months & 1 year. Do not forget to fix the pricing mechanism and also add a penalty clause for short supply/supply failure.
l.	Ancillary resources – contracts for fuel supply	Phase 1	20.05.2020			

Continued...

		Phase	Date				
m.	Ancillary resources – equipment purchase & delivery	Phase 1	25.05.2020				
n.	Ancillary resources – contracts for transportation (centralised kitchen)	Phase 1	25.05.2020		Include a clause for increased requirement after 6 months & 1 year. Do not forget to fix the pricing mechanism and also add a penalty clause for transportation failure.		
	Allocate responsibilities to different staff	Phase 1	28.05.2020				
	GO-LIVE	**Phase 1**	**01.06.2020**				

Follow the same process for a Phase 2, Phase 3 & achievement of the Root cause solution.

Budget for Seminar/ Conference (3 Day Event)

Incomes	No.	Rate	Amount	TOTAL	Expenditure	No.	Rate	Amount	TOTAL
I. Registration Fees				322500.00	I. Food & refreshments				285000.00
a. At regular rate of Rs. 250 per day x 3 days	400	250	300000		Breakfast/Lunch/dinner expenses (450 Participans + 50 volunteers X 3 Days)	500	150	225000	
b. 50 Early bird registrations at the rate of Rs. 200 per day x 3 days	50	150	22500		Tea & Snacks (450 Participans + 50 volunteers X 3 Days x 2 times)	500	20	60000	
c. Others	0	0	0						
					II. Stage & Venue Hire				90,600.00
					Stage Backdrop	1	10000	10000	
					Lights for Decorations	100	100	10000	
II. Corporate sponsorships				50000.00	Stage Setup cost per day (chairs, etc) (3 days)	20	10	600	

Item	No.	Rate	Amount	Item	No.	Rate	Amount
Banners	10	5000	50000	Hire of venue per day including chairs for 500 persons x 3 days	3	20000	60000
Others	0	0	0	Miscellaneous expenses on venue	1	10000	10000
III. Donations			105000	**III. Presentations**			55,000.00
a. From Club members	25	3000	75000	Presentations for speakers	20	2000	40000
b. From area/local people	10	1000	10000	Gifts for organising committee	20	500	10000
c. General Donations	10	2000	20000	Certificates for Participants & volunteers	500	10	5000
IV. Souvenir advertisements			110000.00	**IV. Advertisement**			44,500.00
a. Half Page advertisements	30	2000	60000	Printing of souvenir	500	65	32500
				Transport costs for obtaining advertisements	1	10000	10000

Continued...

Particulars				Total
b. Full page advertisement	10	5000	50000	
Printing of ad forms	1000	2	2000	30,000.00
V. Transport & Conveyance				
Transportation for Resource persons/Guest speakers	20	500	10000	
Miscellaneous Conveyance	1	20000	20000	
				8,900.00
VI. Printing & Stationery				
Printing of registration forms	800	3	2400	
Printing of Posters	50	15	750	
Letters & Correspondence	50	5	250	
Photocopying expenses	500	1	500	

Printing & binding of seminar booklet	500	10	5000	45,000.00
VII. Miscellaneous Expenses & Contingences				
Miscellaneous expenses	1	5000	5000	
Contingencies	1	40000	40000	
TOTAL EXPENDITURE				**559,000.00**
TOTAL RECEIPTS				587500.00
Projected Surplus/Deficit				28,500.00

About the Author

Cordell Ashley Payne, is an alumnus of St. Xavier's College (Calcutta) and a qualified Finance professional (MBA-Finance & IT and PGDFA[ICFAI]). He has almost 2 decades of professional experience, spanning the banking industry and the NGO sector and has spent almost equal time working in both sectors of the economy, including being a Branch Manager with HDFC Bank Ltd., working in a senior role with The Assembly of God Church (Calcutta) and also as former Finance Officer for Christian Medical College (Ludhiana), as well as being an NGO board member for several years. With a skill-set covering management, leadership, administration, team-building. team management, planning, foreign exchange, banking, statutory compliances, FCRA, accounts, finance, foreign donors and more, he brings a unique perspective to the Indian NGO sector.

In this book he contrasts the different managerial & operational styles of both sectors and offers practical guidelines to bridge the managerial gaps between the two, thereby building stable NGOs for maximum impact.

He lives in Kolkata (Calcutta), India and can be reached on: deriskingthengo@gmail.com

Acknowledgements

I would personally like to thank the following people, without whom this book would not have seen the light of day.

- My wife (Lancy Maria) and Shibani Gomes (mother-in-law) for doing double duty in keeping my daughter (Alexa) occupied and thereby provide me with sufficient time to complete this book.

- Melissa Payne (my sister) for being the proverbial 'English teacher' and proof reading the book, and weeding out any grammatical errors.

- My parents (Esme & Horace Payne) for the values-based upbringing combined with an emphasis on English, reading, and inculcating in us the dedication to achieve our goals.

Last but definitely not least, *the 'author' of my 'life-book', God Himself,* for the ability and the understanding and the career experiences, to make this book possible.

Thank you, all!